Blessings, Beaches, & Bluebirds

Summer Devotionals Inspired by God's Creation

Blessings, Beaches, & Bluebirds

Summary Devotionals Inspired by God's Creation

ANDREA ROBINSON

McGahan

Blessings, Beaches, & Bluebirds: Summer Devotionals Inspired by God's Creation

Rooted & Flourishing Devotional Series

McGahan Publishing House | Lynchburg, Tennessee

www.mphbooks.com

Requests for information should be sent to:

info@mphbooks.com

————————————————

Cover Design by Marynn Spurlock & Andrew Waters

Photos & Graphics by Kaleigh Madison LLC

ISBN 978-1-951252-28-1

For Dylan and Lilly, my precious nephew

and niece

Contents

Acknowledgements

As always, I'm overwhelmed by the love and support of the people God has placed in my life. Words can't express the extent to which I am thankful for my family and friends. To Wesley, you are my North Star, soulmate, and best friend. From emotional support to devotional feedback to household upkeep, I couldn't function without you. I'm honored that you've taken time out of your busy days to read every devotional in the whole series. My writing is certainly better because of your feedback. To Asher, my favorite surprise and faithful assistant, thank you for remaining patient and peaceful despite my frenetic pace. Your attention to detail and organizational skills equip me to accomplish exponentially more than I could alone. To Abel, the life of the party and heart of our family, your love keeps my priorities in order and gives me the confidence to reach goals beyond my imagination. To my parents, Gary and Debra, your quiet, calm strength encourages and inspires me always. To Ben and Ginger, I love doing life together, and to Dylan and Lilly, being your aunt has blessed me beyond measure. I can't wait to see the amazing plans God has in store for your lives! To my dear friends Tom and Lisa Buckle and Doug and Melissa Sittason, your support strengthens me more than you know, and my life is enriched because you are part of it. To the many beloved friends who've supported the launch of Rooted and Flourishing—Amanda, Angel, Amy, Barbara, Bridget, Brittani, Hollie, Jessy, Kim, Laura, Lynn, Tonya, Mike—I'm honored by your faith in these devotionals and your willingness to share them with others. To my graphic designer/photographer/media expert, Kaleigh McGinn, I'm thankful for your endless patience and awed at your ability to make my wild ideas look professional. For Caleb Poston and McGahan Publishing, I want to express sincere gratitude once again. Your dialogue and feedback have brought my vision for these devotionals to life and made them better along the way. Finally, thank you to Jesus, my Lord and Friend. I pray that my own imperfect efforts honor you and edify your people.

Introduction & Instructions

Hello friends,

If you read the autumn, winter, or spring volumes of *Rooted &
Flourishing*, I hope you feel like you're returning to spend time with a
friend. With each devotional I write, I imagine sharing my stories with
you face-to-face, and I pray for God to work in your heart. While this
may be your first, second, or third book in the series, this summer
volume is the fourth and final volume for me. I feel as though we've
been growing together for many months, and I pray that as I enter a
brief season of rest, these devotionals will likewise refresh you in the
presence of the Lord.

In case this is the first book you're reading in the *Rooted & Flourishing series*, let me briefly introduce myself. I am a wife, mom, pastor,
scholar, adventurer, fitness fanatic, and avid gardener. I'm far from
perfect, but I love Jesus, I love to learn, and I seize every day with joy.
Despite my qualifications as a scholar, I'm quite irresponsible and im-
pulsive. Nonetheless, God allows me to serve Him in ways that
astound me.

In January 2020 as I was fasting, I felt God compelling me to
write a series of devotions inspired by nature. Although I was excited
about the prospect of writing devotionals, I simply wasn't sure when
I would have time to write them. As a pastor, wife, and mom of two
boys, my schedule didn't exactly provide large blocks of writing time.

Unbeknownst to me, God was already orchestrating the circumstances under which I would be writing devotionals on a daily basis.

As we now know, 2020 was the year in which we encountered the coronavirus, a quarantine, and an unprecedented degree of isolation. In an effort to encourage our church family, our church staff decided to produce daily devotionals, and I lead the project. Initially, I didn't make the connection between the devotionals God was calling me to write and the devotionals I was writing for our church. As time passed, however, I realized that God was helping me sow the seeds of my devotional project.

You now hold in your hands the summer installment of the *Rooted & Flourishing* series. Although many of the devotionals in this volume are inspired by the natural world, we'll also discuss deep topics, such as the relationship between faith and science and the nature of heaven. As you read devotions about our God and the world he created, I pray that you become more deeply rooted in his presence and flourish in your life's journey.

Before you begin, allow me to offer a few suggestions. Each day, I've provided a devotional, a brief prayer, and a prompt for reflection, meditation, or application. I pray that each will serve as a launching point for further prayer, introspection, and growth. In some instances, I've recommended a passage of Scripture or an additional resource for further reading, and in those cases a QR code has been provided for convenient access to the material. For all Scripture passages cited in the devotionals, I've used the New Living Translation with the exception of verses I translated myself.

I've also included blank space for journaling. I will occasionally suggest journaling cues, but the space is primarily for you to write your thoughts on how the devotional impacted you or truths God is impressing upon your soul. As you pray, meditate, and journal, take time to listen for the still, small voice of God. Give him permission to uproot any weeds in the garden of your life, create fertile soil for new growth, and plant the seeds of his will.

— Andrea

Be sure to connect with me at **www.AndreaLeighRobinson.org** and on social media. I have additional content and interactive opportunities waiting for you!

Day 1
Seeds of a New Season

Life flows in seasons, and summer has blossomed! I love everything about the warm months, even the fierce Alabama heat. I eagerly anticipate trips to the beach and weekends at the lake. I delight in watching my bluebirds build their nests and raise their hatchlings. I relish long bike rides in the blazing sunshine. I savor the fresh vegetables and fruits from my garden. I even love working to the point of exhaustion in my yard. I receive each gift the warm weather brings with joy, and I thank my Father for each.

The natural world reminds us that change is an inevitable blessing from our Father. And just as we plant, water, and prune our gardens, we must likewise tend to the garden of our souls. If we want a deeply rooted and flourishing garden, we must be intentional about caring for it, and the changing season creates an opportunity to start afresh.

If we aren't careful, we can become so immersed in our daily routines that we neglect the health of our souls and bodies. We go through the motions and get our work done, yet neglect the aspects of our life that are most important: our relationships, our health, and our spiritual growth.

The prophet Hosea advises proactive measures: "Plant the good seeds of righteousness, and you will harvest a crop of love. Plow up the hard ground of your hearts, for now is the time to seek the Lord, that he may come and shower righteousness upon you," (Hosea 10:12).

As we journey through the summer together, we'll heed Hosea's advice, plow the soil of our souls, and plant seeds of righteousness. We'll discuss virtues such as self-control, generosity, compassion, and holiness, while seeking to prune undesirable weeds such as pride, bitterness, and complacency.

The changing season creates an opportunity for self-reflection, gratitude, and growth. Let's ask our Father to prepare our hearts for whatever he desires to plant, prune, or uproot. As we seek his face and listen for his voice, let's be diligent to tend our gardens as he directs.

Father, thank you for working in my life in every season. I ask you to uproot anything that is cluttering the garden of my heart. Plant seeds of righteousness so that I will reap a harvest of love and joy. Teach me to cultivate health in my soul and body so that I can fulfill your calling for my life. Empower me to nourish the people you have placed around me from the overflow of my own health. Reveal specific areas in which you would have me grow in this coming season. In Jesus' name, Amen.

Personal Reflection

Prayerfully reflect on the condition of your heart. Organize your thoughts into two lists below. What might God be calling you to uproot or prune in the next season of life, and what seeds might he be leading you to plant or cultivate?

_____

_____

_____

_____

_____

Day 2
The Early Bird Gets the Mealworm

In a spring devotional, I introduced you to the bluebird family that nests on my back fence each spring and summer. I delight in watching them build their nest, lay eggs, and raise hatchlings. I enjoy them so much that I've taken measures to make my yard more inviting for them. First, I added a second birdhouse in case any additional bluebird families might like to move in. Next, I did a bit of research and learned that bluebirds prefer to have a water source near their home. Thus, I purchased two birdbaths—one for each birdhouse.

I also learned that bluebirds' favorite food is mealworms. Although I find mealworms utterly disgusting, my love for the bluebirds is greater than my revulsion toward the worms. So, I purchased two feeders specifically designed for mealworms, as well as the worms to inhabit the feeders. I must be honest and admit that I made Wesley, my husband, set out the live worms, but I still felt proud of my self-sacrifice. Needless to say, my bluebirds absolutely relished their new treats, and a second family of bluebirds moved into the additional house!

On a more serious note, the authors of Scripture teach us to foster selflessness as we imitate the model of Jesus. Paul teaches, "Do nothing from selfishness or vain conceit, but with humility regard one another above yourselves; not looking out for yourself only, but for each other. Have this mindset in you, which was also in Christ Jesus," (Philippians 2:3–4, my translation). Our Savior modeled sacrificial love throughout his time on this earth to the point that he forfeited his life on our behalf.

Although self-denial is contrary to our instinct, God knows that selfishness only leads to discontentment. When we live for self, nothing satisfies the soul. Yet, if we sacrifice our own wants and desires, we gain lasting fulfillment and joy. The principal doesn't make logical sense, but even secular studies reveal that living for a greater purpose yields lasting contentment while self-absorption fosters depression.

When we cultivate the mindset of Christ through sacrificial service, we nurture our own soul. Even better, we get to bring healing and hope to our loved ones, our communities, and our world. We might not transform into a saint overnight, but as we practice selflessness moment by moment, we become more like our Lord every day. We might even reap the rewards of our self-sacrifice with a few new bluebirds of blessing!

Jesus, thank you for modeling a life of selfless love, and thank you for redeeming my soul. Teach me to cultivate a mindset of humility and service as I seek to be transformed into your image. I repent of ignoring the needs of others and hoarding the resources with which you have blessed me. Give me the self-discipline to overcome my selfish desires and the strength to serve my fellow humans. Help me see others through your eyes and give me a desire to share your grace. In your name, Amen.

Personal Reflection

Practice self-denial and sacrificial service today. Look for opportunities to bless others and extend kindness, even when it might be inconvenient for you.

_____

_____

Day 3

Day 3
Hungry Hatchlings

Yesterday we discussed the bluebirds that nest in my yard each spring and summer. I delight in watching them because they're beautiful, but also because they teach me life lessons.

Each year, after the birds complete their new nest, they lay a clutch of eggs and soon hatch babies. The hatchlings can't fly for several weeks, so mom and dad bluebird must bring them food. And like most small birds, bluebird babies need to eat constantly to stay alive. Thus, every few minutes, over the course of several weeks, mom and dad bluebird deliver food to their hatchlings. Let me reiterate that just in case you missed it - the adult birds deliver food every few minutes over the course of several weeks!

The first summer I noticed this pattern, I started to feel sorry for the bluebirds. Weren't they worn out? Weren't they sick of flying back and forth, searching for seeds and worms? Weren't they frustrated by the constant shrieks of their hungry babies? But then God gently spoke to my heart and said, "The bluebirds are doing what I created them to do."

Paul teaches a similar principle in Philippians. The apostle exhorts, "God is working in you, giving you the desire and the power to do what pleases him," (Philippians 2:13). When we live according to the plans and purposes of God, we are energized. As Jesus says in Matthew 11:28, "My yoke is easy to bear, and the burden I give you is light." God's calling on each of our lives is a blessing, not a burden.

Only when we step outside of God's will and go our own way does life become exhausting.

When we are yoked with Christ and moving in the direction he leads, he helps carry our burdens. If we slip the yoke off or pull in a different direction, however, we take the entire burden upon our own shoulders. Jesus hasn't left us; we've walked away from him.

When we accept God's calling, whatever that may be, he gives us both the strength and the desire to fulfill it. Our calling might seem tedious to another person, but God has uniquely suited us to walk with him down that path. Feeding those bluebird babies looks tedious to me, but mom and dad bluebird are perfectly content because they are operating according to God's perfect plan. In a similar way, God has a perfect plan for your life, and he will provide you with the desire, power, and motivation to fulfill his plan.

Father, Thank you for equipping me to fulfill your calling. I pray that you would help me discern your purpose for my current season of life and walk in obedience. Guide and direct me onto the path you have chosen. Give me the power and the desire to fulfill your calling. I ask that you take away any rebellious desires in my heart, and I repent of going my own way. I know that your plans are for good and that you have wonderful blessings in store for me. In Jesus' name, Amen.

Personal Reflection

Prayerfully meditate on your life's purpose. What overarching calling might God might be impressing upon you? Write down your thoughts then consider whether your daily priorities align with your God-given purpose. If you aren't sure, make time to talk with a spiritual mentor or pastor.

Day 4
Showers of Blessing — Part 1

The last couple of days, we talked about the bluebirds that reside in my yard during the warm months. Although they aren't domesticated, I consider them my pets, at least during the spring and summer. I care for them as much as possible without scaring them away, and I monitor their condition regularly.

Thus, one rainy afternoon, I was concerned for their wellbeing. I felt sympathy for the poor birds who were, from my perspective, suffering in the rain. As I thought about my birds, the following passage came to mind: "For [God] gives his sunlight to both the evil and the good, and he sends rain on the just and the unjust alike," (Matthew 5:45). I envisioned my birds like the righteous people in this verse, facing hardship despite their innocence.

On a surface level, I've always understood the "rain" in this passage as a trial, something that the righteous don't deserve. Indeed, in our culture, rain is often viewed as gloomy and depressing. On a practical level, rain gets my feet wet, it gets my truck dirty, and it makes my yard muddy. Not to mention, my spoiled dogs hate going outside to do their business in the rain.

So, I went outside to check on my birds. I hoped to catch a glimpse but expected them to be sequestered away in their nests. However, the little creatures were literally singing in the rain. They were chirping, hopping in puddles, shaking their feathers, and feeding their babies as usual.

The behavior of the birds prompted me to reassess my understanding of the previous scripture. I set out to examine more verses about rain, and I was reminded that in the Bible, rain is a blessing from God! In the dry desert climate of Israel, especially in the days before irrigation and technology, people needed rain to survive. If they didn't get rain, their crops would die, and they would starve!

God showed me that I had been understanding Matthew 5:45 the wrong way. When God promises to send rain on the just and the unjust, he is saying that he loves to bless people. In fact, he is such a loving God that he even blesses those who reject him.

Just as the rain was a blessing to the ancient peoples of Palestine, rain is also a blessing to you and me. Even though we aren't as directly involved in agriculture, rain is still required for food to grow. Rain nourishes the ecosystems of the natural world, replenishes freshwater supplies needed for life, and provides energy for hydroelectric power.

I wondered how had I, a gardener, misinterpreted such an obvious blessing? As I pondered my interpretive misstep, I began to wonder what other blessings I might be overlooking in my life. We'll return to this passage tomorrow, but for now, let's pause to thank God for his showers of blessing!

Father, thank you for showering abundant blessings upon my life. Open my eyes to your generosity and kindness. I repent of grumbling and complaining when circumstances aren't exactly as I desire. Empower me to reassess my trials so I can see how you are blessing me through them. Teach me to live with a heart full of gratitude in every season. In Jesus' name, Amen.

Personal Reflection

Are there any areas of your life or any situations that you have been viewing as a hardship that might actually be a blessing in disguise? Attune your heart to God and open your eyes to look for God's blessings all around you, even in the less desirable areas.

Day 5
Showers of Blessing — Part 2

Yesterday we discussed my bluebirds' enjoyment of the rain. Although we tend to dislike rain showers and consider them an inconvenience, rain is actually a blessing from God. Jesus teaches, "For [God] gives his sunlight to both the evil and the good, and he sends rain on the just and the unjust alike," (Matthew 5:45).

As I shared yesterday, God helped me understand that the rain in this verse isn't a punishment, but a blessing. When God promises to send rain on the just and the unjust, he is proclaiming that he loves to bless his people. In fact, he is such a loving God that he even blesses those who reject him.

The surrounding verses confirm this interpretation. Jesus exhorts, "But I say, love your enemies! Pray for those who persecute you! . . . If you love only those who love you, what reward is there for that? Even corrupt tax collectors do that much. If you are kind only to your friends, how are you different from anyone else? Even pagans do that. But you are to be perfect, even as your Father in heaven is perfect," (Matthew 5:44, 46–48). Our Father loves all people, and we are called to reflect his character. Jesus exhorts us to love even those who do us harm, not just those who are easy to love. We will never "be perfect" as our Father is perfect, but our Savior challenges us to strive for his compassionate standard.

We typically think of this principle as a distinctively New Testament concept, as if the God of the Old Testament softened his stance toward sinners once Jesus was born. However, in Leviticus 19:18, God commands, "Love your neighbor as yourself. I am the Lord." God's call for his people to reflect his loving character is a foundational concept throughout Scripture. As his children, we are called to bless our brothers and sisters, even those we find less than lovable.

Father, thank you for extending your love and grace toward me. Help me reflect your character toward the difficult people in my life. Fill my heart with compassion, and empower me to extend your love. Forgive my hurtful words and actions and help me to likewise forgive those who've harmed me. Reveal practical ways I can show kindness, and give me opportunities to bless my enemies. In Jesus' name, Amen.

Personal Reflection

Seek to bless the people in your life who require extra grace today. Brainstorm a few practical ways you can show love to the unlovely.

_____

_____

_____

_____

_____

_____

_____

_____

Day 6
Dangerous Dogs

Summer is prime bike riding season, and I'm an avid road biker. The sun on my shoulders, the wind in my face, and the freedom of peaceful country roads refresh my spirit like nothing else. Road biking, however, is accompanied by a few unique hazards. The biggest danger is, obviously, cars, so I stick to low-traffic roads. I've also affixed flashing lights to the front and rear of my bike.

The next greatest danger, believe it or not, is dogs. Something about a bicycle and its rider simply drives a dog insane. I personally know several riders who've sustained life-threatening injuries from dog-related bike wrecks. Thus, most serious bikers carry pepper spray in case an angry canine decides to attack.

I'll share my strategy for handling dogs, but please note that I am not recommending you try it. Although I have pepper spray affixed to my handlebars, it's never been used. I've encountered many dogs on deserted country roads, but none have ventured to attack. When a dog begins to bark and chase, most bikers yell and try to scare the dog away, which only incites the dog to further aggression. Instead, my tactic is to speak soothing words to the dog as if it were my own beloved pup. Usually, the dog will stop barking, slow down, and tilt its head with a puzzled expression on its furry face. Again, I'm not recommending you try this strategy, but in over 20 years of road biking, no dog has ever nipped at my heels.

In our interactions with other humans, we often go on the offensive or become needlessly defensive. What if, instead, we responded to tense situations with kindness and serenity? Peter recommends, "Don't retaliate with insults when people insult you. Instead, pay them back with a blessing. That is what God has called you to do, and he will grant you his blessing," (1 Peter 3:9). When we respond with gentleness, we can diffuse a difficult situation more often than not. Instead of inciting further conflict, we create an opportunity for anger to cool and frustration to dissipate.

As Peter promises, our measured and thoughtful response reaps an immediate blessing. As we honor our Father by controlling our emotions and taming our tongue, we are spared the strain of fractured relationships and wounded feelings. We also bless our peers by helping them maintain their equilibrium. Instead of deteriorating into conflict, the situation can become an avenue for healing and productive dialogue. Although I don't advise that you try my strategy with angry dogs, I highly recommend Peter's strategy with angry people!

Father, thank you for giving me the capacity to control my emotions and my tongue. Help me continually grow in both areas. I pray that my interactions with others would be defined by grace and peace. Give me the strength to maintain my equilibrium even when I am faced with insults and enmity. Teach me to respond with kindness instead of reacting in anger. Empower me to reflect your character as I seek to bless even those who hurt me. In Jesus' name, Amen.

Personal Reflection

Over the next few days, give extra attention to interactions that are tense or heated. Practice responding with kindness and gentleness instead of reacting in anger. Just like any skill, the more you practice, the more progress you'll make.

_____

_____

_____

_____

_____

_____

_____

_____

_____

_____

_____

_____

_____

_____

_____

_____

Day 7
Parched — Part 1

Here in Alabama, we've reached the season of brutal heat and humidity. Doing anything outdoors can be extremely uncomfortable, and simply walking outside causes me to sweat. So, if I want to ride my bike in the hot Alabama sun, I have to carefully plan and prepare. Most importantly, I load up with as much water as possible. So far, the most I've been able to pack is 5 liters, and in the summer heat, I consume every drop.

After one particularly thirsty bike ride, I felt the Lord nudging my heart about the idea of thirst. The Father brought Psalm 63:1 to my mind: "You, God, are my God, earnestly I seek you; I thirst for you, my whole being longs for you, in a dry and parched land where there is no water." When we're in a dry and parched land, our body gets thirsty. Similarly, when we face trials and challenges, our soul thirsts for relief.

The longing for spiritual refreshing is normal and even beneficial as long as we turn to our Father to quench our thirst. If, however, we don't quench our thirst upon God and his Word, we'll try to quench it with the wrong things, such as unhealthy relationships, bad habits, or harmful substances.

Although we all seek relief in different ways, only God can truly satiate our deepest longings. He might not take away our trials, but he can refresh our souls in the midst of trials, providing relief from anxiety, frustration, and anger.

And just as we need fresh water every single day, we need living water from our Father on a regular basis. Just as one sip of water won't suffice for the whole day, we need to stay connected to God all day long. We should spend time with God in the morning and consult him on every decision throughout the day. We should express gratitude for every blessing and pray with those going through their own trials. We should pray with our family at bedtime and invite God to be part of our homes (Deuteronomy 6:4–9).

In short, we must consume his living water at every opportunity, and never let ourselves become so parched that we are tempted to consume a sub-par substitute. Let's prepare for each day more diligently than I prepare for a bike ride in the hot Alabama sun.

Father, thank you for refreshing my soul when I feel parched and dry. Teach me to quench my spiritual thirst on your presence so that I'm not tempted to indulge in substitutes that will never satisfy my soul. I repent of neglecting time in prayer and Bible study. Give me the perseverance to seek you not just each morning but throughout every day. Help me create habits and routines that facilitate quality time with you. In Jesus' name, Amen.

Personal Reflection

Prayerfully consider how you seek to refresh your spirit when you feel stressed, worried, or tired. Are you intentional to seek God and engage in pursuits that foster health? Or do you revert to quick and easy substitutes that bring short-term pleasure, but long-term harm? Write your thoughts below so you can reference them tomorrow.

Day 7

_____

_____

_____

_____

_____

_____

_____

_____

_____

_____

_____

_____

_____

_____

_____

_____

_____

Day 8
Parched — Part 2

When physical and environmental conditions are taxing, we realize that water is vital, and we long for it desperately. Our Lord intentionally uses water as a metaphor to describe our need for him. So, today I would like to focus on some of the qualities of water that make hydration so desirable and essential.

First, water sustains life. As I'm sure you know, our physical bodies can't survive long without water. Initially, we get tired and weak. As we grow more dehydrated, however, our brain begins to shut down so that we can't think clearly. Eventually, our muscles fail, our organs fail, and our body dies.

Similarly, without God our spirits become weak, and we have trouble making wise decisions. Our joy shrivels and our peace withers. Even though we remain physically alive, we begin to feel dead inside. Thus, just as actual water sustains us, God's living water helps us enjoy a fulfilling life.

Second, water not only sustains; it purifies. When we drink water, toxins and impurities are washed from our bodies. Likewise, Jesus washes away our sins, and the Holy Spirit helps us live in increasing purity. He continually convicts us of harmful thoughts and habits, then helps us make better choices. Thus, the more we drink of God's presence, the more pure, holy, and wise we become.

Third, water energizes. As we drink, water delivers essential nutrients to the cells in our body. Muscle cells, in particular, require nutrients to produce energy. Similarly, our time with God in prayer and Bible study empowers and motivates us. God created us for a purpose, and he reveals that purpose when we spend time with him. As we allow him to guide and direct us in small daily decisions, he empowers us to move forward with increasing power and purpose.

The bottom line is that we must consume living water every day to obtain the benefits our Lord wants to provide. Fortunately, Jesus offers an endless supply of living water, and he longs to refresh his people. According to John 7:37–38, "Jesus stood and shouted to the crowds, 'Anyone who is thirsty may come to me! Anyone who believes in me may come and drink!'" Let's accept his gracious offer and drink deeply.

Jesus, thank you for pouring yourself out so that I can experience an abundant life. Teach me to quench my thirst on your presence instead of turning to temporary substitutes that will spiritually dehydrate me. I repent of trying to refresh myself with harmful habits. Help me develop a lifestyle of abiding in your presence. I pray that my life would be so saturated in your love that I would be an agent of refreshing for others. In your name, Amen.

Personal Reflection

Review your thoughts from yesterday and identify any harmful habits with which you are trying to refresh your soul. Write them below so that you can return to them tomorrow.

_____

_____

_____

Day 9
Watermelon

The last couple of days we've talked about refreshing our souls on the life-giving water of God. We discussed being intentional to seek his presence daily, and we sought to identify and eliminate earthly substitutes that will further dehydrate our souls. Today I'd like to talk about practical strategies for remaining spiritually hydrated. But first, allow me to share my favorite way to stay hydrated during hot Alabama summers.

No matter how much water I drink while biking, I always get dehydrated in the summer months. After a long bike ride, I return home with salt crusted on my clothing from hours of sweating in the heat. As soon as I change out of my sweaty bike gear, I plop down on the patio with a watermelon. I eat until my stomach feels like bursting, and the crisp cool fruit tastes like the dew of heaven. I don't feel guilty for overeating because watermelon is one of the healthiest foods on the planet. The fruit is packed with nutrients, including cancer-fighting antioxidants and heart-healthy amino acids. Watermelon contains vitamins and anti-inflammatory compounds that promote joint, eye, and skin health. It boosts the immune system, improves circulation, and lowers blood pressure. Most important for my bike rides, watermelon replenishes essential electrolytes and reduces muscle soreness. In case you can't tell, I'm *obsessed* with watermelon.

If I'm being honest, I'm not sure anything refreshes my soul as quickly and efficiently as watermelon replenishes my body. But no quick fixes exist for spiritual health, and we must be even more intentional to refresh our souls than our bodies. Just as I make sure my watermelon is ready and waiting for me *before* I ride my bike, we must be purposeful about putting strategies in place to keep our spirits hydrated with the living water of God. Some strategies are obvious, like Bible study, prayer, and worship. However, if I can continue to be honest, during the really difficult seasons of life, spiritual disciplines can feel like yet another drain on our tired souls. (Maybe it's just me, but I'll bet you've felt similarly at some point in your life.) So, in addition to maintaining the health of our souls through spiritual disciplines, we must employ strategies that hydrate the parched areas of our soul. For example, spending time in nature refreshes my soul nearly as much as watermelon refreshes my body. No matter what is going on in my life, spending time in the garden, at the beach, or in the woods nourishes my spirit.

Before we close, let me point out that such means of refreshing aren't *in addition to* or *outside of* finding refreshing in the Lord. As we relax into activities we love, our nerves calm, the world quiets, and we begin to hear the gentle voice of our Father. In fact, God is the only true source of refreshment and nourishment. In the familiar words of David,

As the deer longs for streams of water,
so I long for you, O God.
I thirst for God, the living God.
When can I go and stand before him?

. . .

Why am I discouraged?
Why is my heart so sad?
I will put my hope in God!

I will praise him again—
my Savior and my God!
Psalm 42:1–2, 11

When we quench our thirst on the presence of God, he transforms our discouragement into hope and sadness into praise. Just remember that there are no spiritual watermelons that will instantaneously refresh our souls. We must drink deeply of his presence every day and strategically refresh our souls on a regular basis.

Father, thank you for refreshing my soul and spirit when I turn to you. Give me the discipline to spend time in prayer and Bible study every day. Also help me identify activities that lift my spirit and bring joy to my heart. Teach me to draw closer to you as I engage in pursuits that I enjoy. Train me to quiet my mind so that I can hear your still, small voice. I ask you to away any desire to quench my thirst on the false substitutes that this world offers. I pray that I would be able to serve you more faithfully and efficiently as I foster practices that keep my soul healthy. In Jesus' name, Amen.

Personal Reflection

Review your list of harmful habits and false avenues of refreshing from yesterday. Identify a healthier version or a replacement for each that will draw you closer to God and yield lasting health. Make your new list below.

_____

_____

_____

_____

_____

_____

_____

_____

_____

_____

_____

_____

_____

_____

_____

_____

_____

_____

_____

_____

_____

_____

Day 10
Triathlon Travail

Just as summer is prime bike riding season, summer is also tri-athlon season. Although my knees are too worn out for triathlons these days, I completed quite a few in my younger years. I'd like to tell you about one in particular.

The swim portion of this race took place in the Tennessee river. Although the water was pleasantly cool, I was hot from the exertion, and I became increasingly thirsty. The further I swam, the thirstier I got until temptation overcame my good sense. I took a huge, refresh-ing gulp of river water. In that moment, the water tasted glorious and soothed my thirst. I even completed the race without any negative consequences. Soon after, however, I paid the price. I won't go into detail, but I'll simply say that for the next three days, I was sick to my stomach. I assure you; you don't want more info than that.

James speaks about temptation and the result of succumbing to harmful desires. He teaches, "Temptation comes from our own de-sires, which entice us and drag us away. These desires give birth to sinful actions. And when sin is allowed to grow, it gives birth to death," (James 1:14–15). Just as I was tempted to drink nasty river water, we sometimes desire things that are detrimental to our physical and spiritual health. When we act on such desires, we reap death. I'm thankful I didn't ingest any life-threatening bacteria as a result of my foolish decision. However, my poor choice certainly killed my joy for the next few days. Likewise, sinful desires can lead to the death of inner peace, personal relationships, career opportunities, and spiritual health. In extreme cases, sinful excess can lead to actual death.

Similarly, in the Garden of Eden, God warned Adam, "You may freely eat the fruit of every tree in the garden—except the tree of the knowledge of good and evil. If you eat its fruit, you are sure to die," (Genesis 2:16b–17). Although Adam and Eve didn't die physically when they gave into the temptation of eating the forbidden fruit, they lost their home, their innocence, their peace, and their fellowship with God. Our Father, however, desires that we enjoy a life of inner peace and spiritual health. He calls us to unbroken fellowship with him through Jesus Christ. No momentary temptation is worth lasting joy and intimacy with our Savior!

Father, thank you for setting healthy boundaries in my life for the purpose of protection. Empower me to reject any temptations that draw me away from your presence. Give me a greater desire to live in health and wholeness. Help me be wise to the schemes of the Enemy when he tries to tempt me onto paths of destruction. Teach me to recognize my areas of weakness so that I can take proactive measures to walk in obedience. In Jesus' name, Amen.

Personal Reflection

Prayerfully meditate on any areas of temptation or weakness in your life. If you've allowed your temptation to grow into full-blown sin, it's never too late to repent and turn back to your Father. Whether you are struggling with sin or temptation, pray and ask God to help you identify and implement proactive strategies to overcome your weakness.

Day 10

_____

_____

_____

_____

_____

_____

_____

_____

_____

_____

_____

_____

_____

_____

_____

_____

Day 11
Base Building

In cycling, running, and other cardiovascular sports, strategic training can help us increase speed, improve endurance, and achieve goals. Base building, in particular, is one strategy essential to improving performance. If you'll allow me to delve briefly into physiology, I'll get to the spiritual application shortly.

The body operates on three energy systems. The two most powerful systems, the ATP-PC and glycolytic, provide less than ten seconds and two minutes of work, respectively. That won't get us very far! Yet, rookie athletes and amateur fitness enthusiasts often train at the highest possible intensities, rapidly fatiguing the body with quick bursts of energy. Such a strategy may feel rewarding in the moment, but training this way will exhaust our muscles quickly and hinder our long-term goals.

On the other hand, training the aerobic energy system helps us achieve greater output for longer periods of time. Unlike the two anaerobic systems, the aerobic, or oxidative, system can sustain hours of hard work. So, training in our oxidative range, or "building our base" allows us to train with greater efficiency for greater periods of time. Even better, as we build our base, we train the body to remain in the aerobic system for as long as possible, only verging into the anaerobic systems for short bursts when necessary, thus minimizing fatigue. In short, building our base enables us to maximize our potential and power.

In a similar manner, building our spiritual foundation empowers us to serve God with more effectiveness and longevity. The Apostle Peter offers a list of basics by which we can fortify our foundation. He teaches,

> By his divine power, God has given us everything we need for living a godly life. We have received all of this by coming to know him, the one who called us to himself by means of his marvelous glory and excellence. And because of his glory and excellence, he has given us great and precious promises. These are the promises that enable you to share his divine nature and escape the world's corruption caused by human desires. In view of all this, make every effort to respond to God's promises. Supplement your faith with a generous provision of moral excellence, and moral excellence with knowledge, and knowledge with self-control, and self-control with patient endurance, and patient endurance with godliness, and godliness with brotherly affection, and brotherly affection with love for everyone.

2 Peter 1:3–7

To recap, Peter encourages us to cultivate moral excellence, knowledge, self-control, patience, endurance, godliness, and brotherly affection. That's a tall order! But remember that we are building our base, and we don't have to master everything all at once. Just as we build our physical fitness a little at a time, we grow spiritually day by day. And through training the basics, we grow perseverance, discipline, and maturity rather than burning ourselves out through short bursts of emotionally driven spirituality that lacks a stable foundation.

To extend the analogy further, just as we don't always want to exercise, we must be disciplined to grow in godliness even when we don't feel like it. We are training to battle against the Enemy of this world, and the rewards of training far exceed any temporary discomfort. So, let's maximize our potential and power in the battle to spread the love of Jesus. As Paul teaches, "Run to win! All athletes are disciplined in their training. They do it to win a prize that will fade away, but we do it for an eternal prize. So I run with purpose in every step," (1 Corinthians 9:24b–26a).

Heavenly Father, thank you for equipping me to grow, mature, and thrive in my faith. I repent of neglecting to cultivate the habits and virtues that will empower me to serve you well. I ask you to reveal areas in which I am weak so that I can fortify my foundation. Give me a greater desire to cultivate holiness, knowledge, patience, endurance, and kindness. Teach me to live a disciplined life of faith and obedience. Train me to become a powerful and victorious athlete in your Kingdom. In Jesus' name, Amen.

Personal Reflection

Prayerfully reflect upon Peter's list—holiness, knowledge, patience, endurance, kindness—and choose one virtue to cultivate over the next few weeks. Alternately, if you are weak in other foundational areas, you might begin with one of those instead, i.e., prayer, fellowship, forgiveness, humility, etc. Then, if you are feeling especially motivated, I encourage you to write out a training plan for the next six months in which you focus on a particular virtue or discipline each month. Write your thoughts below.

Day 11

Day 12
Doggy Disobedience

Obedience isn't a topic that gives us a warm, fuzzy feeling. God's commands in Scripture sometimes seem restrictive, harsh, unreasonable, and even arbitrary. Just read some of those crazy regulations in the Torah, like "don't boil a baby goat in its mother's milk," (Exodus 23:19). What?!?

The good news is that we don't have to understand, or even like, all of God's commands. We are, however, called to trust Him. The statutes outlined in Scripture are given for several reasons, and one of those reasons is our protection.

Let me illustrate using my dogs as an example. Smokey and Pepper are energetic, curious, mischievous mini-schnauzers. Since miniature schnauzers were originally bred to be ratters, hunting is in their DNA. They thrive on chasing other animals, digging for treasure (real or imagined), and meeting new people. Yet, because they are bold and adventurous, their potential for getting into trouble is high. Thus, we have a fence around our yard to protect them. The fence prevents my dogs from picking fights with other animals, getting run over by cars, or drowning in the pond, since most mini-schnauzers can't swim.

In a similar scenario with a different fence, we took the dogs to visit the lake house when they were puppies. We enclosed Smokey and Pepper on the gated porch, thinking that we would allow them to enjoy the outdoors without risking their safety. With the dogs secured, the family departed for a ride on the boat and returned a few hours later. When we returned, the dogs had escaped, and Smokey had a broken leg. I was heartbroken, and my precious puppy was in severe pain.

Even worse, we all bore the consequences of his illicit activities. An expensive surgery was required, after which Smokey's movement had to be restricted. For months, my energetic pup had to reside in a small pen inside the house. We hated it as much as Smokey, because multiple times per day, we had to wrap his casted leg in plastic and carry him outside to do his business.

I feel like we often create a similar scenario for ourselves with respect to God's protection. He provides clear boundaries in Scripture, but we feel confined and restricted. Thus, we decide to venture outside the safe perimeter God has outlined. When we inevitably face the consequences of our transgressions, we limp back to God broken and battered. Although our Father is faithful to help us become healthy and whole again, he would prefer that we trust him in the first place.

In Psalm 119, the centerpiece of the entire Bible, the psalmist rejoices over the joy of a life lived in obedience to God. He prays,

> *Teach me your decrees, O Lord;*
> *I will keep them to the end.*
> *Give me understanding and I will obey your instructions;*
> *I will put them into practice with all my heart.*
> *Make me walk along the path of your commands,*
> *for that is where my happiness is found.*
> ### *Psalm 119:33–35*

Our Father desires that we live an abundant and joyful life, and obedience to his commands makes that possible.

If you have a rebellious streak, I can relate. When I see a fence or barrier, my first instinct is to crash through it to see what is on the other side. As I've grown in Christ, however, I've learned to trust Him more and more. I've learned that God's commands aren't given to keep me FROM anything, except maybe trials and heartache. Rather, God's instructions are given FOR my benefit. God has a joyful, abundant life FOR me, and I can only experience it fully through faith and obedience.

Father, thank you for creating healthy boundaries in order to protect me. Teach me to obey your commands even when I don't understand them. I repent of my rebellious tendencies and ask you to bring my heart in alignment with yours. Help me trust that your wisdom is greater than my own. Give me the self-discipline to adhere to your will for my life. Grow my love for you so that my greatest desire is to become more like you. In Jesus' name, Amen.

Personal Reflection

Prayerfully consider whether you are harboring any rebellious tendencies in your heart. Do any of God's Scriptural boundaries chafe against your inclinations? Ask God to replace each desire with an alternative that brings health and holiness to your soul. Write your thoughts below so you can review them tomorrow.

_____

_____

_____

_____

_____

_____

Day 12

_____

_____

_____

_____

_____

_____

_____

_____

_____

_____

_____

_____

_____

_____

_____

_____

_____

Day 13
Horseflies — Part 1

In the spring and summer of 2020, my back patio became my office. Like many people, I worked from home during the pandemic, so I created a workspace outside. Each morning, I began my day with a workout on the patio then transitioned seamlessly into my workday.

One particular morning, I was joined by a massive horsefly. If you aren't familiar, a horsefly is about 50 times the size of a normal fly. But I love nature, so I thought, if he doesn't bother me, I won't bother him. Unfortunately, the horsefly wasn't on board with my unspoken arrangement.

A couple of days later, as I was exercising, I felt a sharp pain on my back. The awful creature had bitten me through my clothes, and it hurt! Before I could take action, he bit me again, this time on my rear! Fortunately, horseflies aren't very quick or agile, so my attacker met a swift demise.

The situation offers a good illustration, however. The Enemy is a bit like that horsefly. We know we shouldn't let him hang around, but we think we are in control. We allow a few "little sins" to be part of our life. We think we have an unspoken agreement with the Enemy, that we'll allow him to have a little ground, but no more. Just like my imaginary agreement with the horsefly, however, our Enemy has not agreed to anything. He will not be content with taking a little bit of ground. He has a plan for our lives, and his plan is not for our benefit. Peter teaches, "Stay alert! Watch out for your great Enemy, the devil.

He prowls around like a roaring lion, looking for someone to devour. Stand firm against him, and be strong in your faith," (1 Peter 5:8–9a). Satan isn't an honorable foe. He'll sneak up, attack us from behind, knock us over, and kick us while we're down. If we know the Enemy wants to kill, steal, and destroy, why would we let him hang around? Why would we give him *any* ground?

Thankfully, we serve a good God who has a perfect plan for our lives. If we trust him and follow his guidance, he will defend us on all sides. When Satan tries to sneak up and bite us, God will be there to protect us. The Enemy can only gain access to our lives if we allow him in. So, let's search out hearts and see if we've allowed any nefarious horseflies to take residence in our lives.

Father, thank you for equipping me to stand firm against the Enemy. Search my heart and reveal whether I have allowed the Enemy to take ground in my life. Teach me to deal with temptations and sins in a swift and decisive manner. Take away my desire to participate in any activity that would harm me or others, even if it seems desirable at the moment. I pray that you would reveal any sins or harmful habits of which I might be unaware so that I can live an abundant and righteous life. In Jesus' name, Amen.

Personal Reflection

Review your notes from yesterday and prayerfully determine whether you need to add any struggle to your list, even "little sins" that might seem insignificant. Identify how each struggle/sin from both yesterday and today has the potential to cause harm in your life. Then consider why you want to purge the sin and how your life will be better as a result. Once again, ask God to replace each desire with an alternative that brings health and holiness to your soul.

Blessings, Beaches, & Bluebirds

Day 14
Horseflies — Part 2

In a couple of spring devotionals, I told you about the massive pumpkin crop that grew spontaneously by my back patio. I'm never one to uproot a good plant, so as the vines started sprouting, I cleared the space of grass, cordoned off the area, and let the pumpkins flourish.

Around the same time, I began to experience an unprecedented number of horseflies on my patio. Having learned from previous experience, I swiftly dispatched each one. Despite my diligence, however, the number of horseflies continued to increase. I simply couldn't figure out where they were coming from—until one atypical morning.

During the hot summer months, my sprinkler system runs in the morning, and I water selectively in the afternoon. For whatever reason, I happened to be manually watering my garden one morning. As I approached the pumpkin vines, I saw that the big, yellow blossoms were filled with horseflies. Apparently the not-so-little pests are lively in the mornings, and their favorite place to party is the pumpkin vine.

I faced a dilemma. I could douse the vines in pesticide, which was not a favorable option because I was looking forward to homemade pumpkin pie in the fall. Alternately, I could uproot the vines completely, also not a favorable option for obvious reasons. Or I could try to coexist with the pests.

As I meditated upon my options, I thought about the nature of unintended consequences. As finite human beings, we almost always make decisions based on incomplete information. Even the wisest person among us can't determine with certainty the outcome of a particular course of action. The prophet Jeremiah teaches,

> *But blessed is the one who trusts in the Lord,*
>
> *whose confidence is in him.*
>
> *They will be like a tree planted by the water*
>
> *that sends out its roots by the stream.*
>
> *It does not fear when heat comes;*
>
> *its leaves are always green.*
>
> *It has no worries in a year of drought*
>
> *and never fails to bear fruit.*
>
> *The heart is deceitful above all things*
>
> *and beyond cure.*
>
> *Who can understand it?*
>
> **Jeremiah 17:7–9**

In sum, we should definitely *not* follow the advice of the 1980's pop hit "Listen to Your Heart." Our Father is the only source of wisdom and stability.

In case you are wondering, I determined that inaction was the least offensive option with my pumpkin plants and horseflies. Although the horseflies were unwelcome, the alternatives were even less desirable. I don't know if prayer would have averted my discomfort with the circumstances, but seeking the guidance of God will definitely help us avoid undesirable outcomes in our life. Let's seek his wisdom in every circumstance, and let God help us avoid those nasty horseflies.

Father, thank you for making your wisdom available to me. Teach me to consult you before every decision, big and small. I repent of going my own way instead of seeking you. Help me trust you to lead and guide me, even when I think I know the best course of action. Grow my roots deeper in you and empower me to discern your voice from among the many others I hear. In Jesus' name, Amen.

Personal Reflection

What decisions are you facing in the forthcoming days, weeks, and months? Make a list below, and remember that no decision is too insignificant. Pray over each choice and commit to follow the direction of the Lord, even if it isn't the direction you want to go.

_____

_____

_____

_____

_____

_____

_____

_____

_____

_____

_____

_____

_____

Day 15
Judge Jephthah

Yesterday we discussed the manner in which our actions tend to incur unintended consequences. We'll stay on that subject today and discuss the tragic narrative of Jephthah.

In the book of Judges, Jephthah was a formidable warrior. He was so renowned that the people of Israel begged him to lead their army against the Ammonites. Despite his initial reluctance, Jephthah eventually agreed and led the people with zeal. The author of the biblical text records,

> At that time the Spirit of the Lord came upon Jephthah, and he went throughout the land of Gilead and Manasseh, including Mizpah in Gilead, and from there he led an army against the Ammonites. And Jephthah made a vow to the Lord. He said, "If you give me victory over the Ammonites, I will give to the Lord whatever comes out of my house to meet me when I return in triumph. I will sacrifice it as a burnt offering."

Judges 11:29–31

Scholars debate whether Jephthah made the foolish vow knowing he might have to sacrifice one of his children, as was a common pagan practice. However, farm animals were often kept within the inner courtyard of a family residence. So, Jephthah might have made his vow expecting an animal to be first out of the gates. Either way, his post-victory grief when his daughter emerged implies that the outcome was not the one for which he had hoped. The author records,

> *When Jephthah returned home to Mizpah, his daughter came out to meet him, playing on a tambourine and dancing for joy. She was his one and only child; he had no other sons or daughters. When he saw her, he tore his clothes in anguish. "Oh, my daughter!" he cried out. "You have completely destroyed me! You've brought disaster on me! For I have made a vow to the Lord, and I cannot take it back."*

Judges 11:34–35

Shortly thereafter, the narrative ends with the sacrifice and death of Jephthah's daughter (Judges 11:39).

Jephthah's vow was foolish, and the consequences he reaped were tragic. As a flawed human with imperfect knowledge, Jephthah made a mistake. On the surface, vowing to offer a victory sacrifice was admirable. However, Jephthah failed to consult the Lord. Had he taken a moment to seek God's direction, he could have avoided calamity.

Hopefully, you already see the application. You and I don't have access to the omniscience of our Father, but we have access to the Father himself. No decision is too big or small to bring before him. He wants to be involved in every detail of our lives, and he'll offer guidance when we seek direction. Even choices that might seem "good" on the surface, like Jephthah's sacrificial pledge, might be outside of God's will. We simply need to ask and find out.

Father, thank you for being a God who is near and for caring about every detail of my life. Teach me to seek your will in every circumstance, big and small. Help me be so immersed in your presence that my automatic response to every situation is to consult you. I pray that I would learn from the example of Jephthah as I seek to offer sacrifices that are truly pleasing to you. In Jesus' name, Amen.

Personal Reflection

Revisit the list you made yesterday. If any other forthcoming decisions come to mind, add those to your notes. Once again, pray over each decision and commit to follow the direction of the Lord, even if it isn't the direction you want to go.

_____

_____

_____

_____

_____

_____

_____

_____

_____

_____

_____

_____

_____

_____

_____

_____

_____

_____

_____

_____

_____

_____

_____

_____

_____

_____

Day 16
A Clean Sweep

As I've mentioned, my back patio became my office during the covid quarantine. I made the space so comfortable, functional, and beautiful, that I've continued to work outside whenever possible. But before I sit down to work, or even exercise on the patio, I always tidy the area. I sweep so often that I have a broom especially designated for the patio. I'm a little obsessive-compulsive about it, but I can't settle in until my patio is clean.

During one of my daily patio sweeps, a strong wind blew grass, dirt, and leaves all over my nearly clean floor. I was quite irked, but I immediately started over and swept until the patio was pristine. Despite my frustration, I realized that God had whispered with the wind: How often do we begin an endeavor, only to encounter a set-back and give up?

We all have hopes and aspirations to become better versions of ourselves. We aspire to cultivate better relationships, become better parents, or foster better friendships. We hope to learn a new skill, improve our health, or draw closer to God. Paul described his efforts to become more like Christ, saying, "I don't mean to say that I have already achieved these things or that I have already reached perfection. But I press on to possess that perfection for which Christ Jesus first possessed me. No, dear brothers and sisters, I have not achieved it, but I focus on this one thing: Forgetting the past and looking forward to what lies ahead," (Philippians 3:12–13). Paul resolved not to let any set-back, mistake, or opposition hinder his progress. And he faced a plethora of obstacles!

The road to success and growth is rarely linear. We almost always experience some type of obstacle, whether it's from within or without. But what if, like Paul, we decided not to let anything get in our way? What if we got back up every time we got knocked down? What if we kept our eyes fixed on Jesus even when we get knocked so far backward that we have to start all over again?

Next time the wind blows dirt all over your clean floor, will you drop your broom and give up? Or will you press ahead, keep sweeping, and grasp every blessing the Lord has in store?

Father, Thank you for helping me grow increasingly into Christ's likeness. Equip me to achieve every purpose and plan you have for my life. Teach me to view obstacles as opportunities, but also help me discern when you are using a set-back to lead me in a different direction. Forgive me for giving up and giving in too easily when you are calling me to press ahead. I ask you to give me a greater measure of endurance and perseverance as I seek to grow more healthy and mature in my faith. In Jesus' name, Amen.

Personal Reflection

Prayerfully meditate on any areas of your life in which you are hoping to grow, improve, or mature. Also review your notes from Day 11, and reassess your goals for growth. Consider whether you are continuing to build your spiritual foundation. What obstacles have you encountered over the last few days and how did you respond? What can you learn from recent or past failures? What practical steps can you implement to increase your potential for success in the future. Write your thoughts below, pray over your ideas, then begin to implement them as the Lord leads you.

Day 16

Day 17

Here Comes the Sun

Every year since I was a little girl, my family has vacationed together at the Florida coast. We love laying on the beach, playing in the water, making sandcastles, going fishing, and searching for sea creatures. However, our trips to the beach require a great deal of preparation. We need swimsuits, beach towels, umbrellas, and chairs. We need sunblock, sunglasses, hats, and aloe vera for the inevitable sunburn. We need coolers, waters, sodas, and snacks. Of course, the supplies aren't absolutely necessary, but they facilitate a fun and enjoyable time.

Can you imagine going to the beach without any supplies? Even worse, can you imagine walking into the desert without sunblock, hats, sunglasses, or any of the supplies that make us comfortable in the sandy heat? We would quickly become sweaty, thirsty, sunburned, and utterly miserable. Now let's continue our theoretical journey through the hot desert, and imagine that a cloud moves over the sun. What relief—blessed shade! But then as the hours pass and evening approaches, a new problem arises. The desert is cold at night, and we can't build a fire because wood is scarce in the desert.

In reality, the likelihood that you or I will find ourselves in such a scenario is almost nonexistent. However, this was the very situation Israel faced when they left Egypt. As the Hebrew men, women, and children traveled through the hot, dry, desert they endured unrelenting sun during the day and freezing desert temps at night. Water was scarce and food was limited.

Day 17

Yet God took care of his people. He not only supplied food and water, but also provided guidance, direction, and protection. Moses records, "The Lord went ahead of them. He guided them during the day with a pillar of cloud, and he provided light at night with a pillar of fire. This allowed them to travel by day or by night. And the Lord did not remove the pillar of cloud or pillar of fire from its place in front of the people," (Exodus 13:21–22).

Similarly, God is prepared to guide you, and the journey before you hasn't taken your Father by surprise. As we'll discuss over the next few days, God is prepared to meet your needs and protect you from harm. Even if you feel as though you are walking through your own personal desert wilderness, the Lord is equipping you, protecting you, and leading you toward your promised land.

Hundreds of years after God led Israel through the desert, the psalmist promises that our Father watches over us with the same attention and care:

He will not let you stumble;
the one who watches over you will not slumber.
Indeed, he who watches over Israel
never slumbers or sleeps.
The Lord himself watches over you!
The Lord stands beside you as your protective shade.
The sun will not harm you by day,
nor the moon at night.
The Lord keeps you from all harm
and watches over your life.
The Lord keeps watch over you as you come and go,
both now and forever.
Psalm 121:3–8

Perhaps you are facing tangible concerns like a loss of job security or physical illness. Perhaps you are navigating emotional turmoil from relational strife or anxiety. Whatever the situation, God is not only with you; he is prepared to meet your needs and protect you from harm. Even better, you and I have an advantage over the Israelites. We don't follow God in a pillar of cloud and fire, we have his very own Spirit dwelling within us (Romans 8:15).

When I was a little girl, I would run and jump into the arms of my Pops. I would close my eyes and snuggle into his strong arms. In those moments, I didn't have a care or worry in the world. I knew he was big enough and strong enough to take care of me.

Whatever the coming days and weeks might bring, remember that your Father is big enough and strong enough to provide exactly what you need.

Father, thank you for watching over me during the day while I am awake and through the night while I'm asleep. Thank you for going before me and protecting me from harm. Teach me to trust you and rest in your love. Help me overcome worry, anxiety, and depression. Give me faith that can't be deterred by the harshest trial because I know that you are with me. Keep my feet firmly on the path you've set before me as I follow you ever closer to my promised land. In Jesus' name, Amen.

Personal Reflection

Instead of focusing on your problems today, think about all the ways God has protected you and provided for you during difficult situations in the past. How might he be protecting you during your current season of life? Write your thoughts below.

Day 17

_____

_____

_____

_____

_____

_____

_____

_____

_____

_____

_____

_____

_____

_____

_____

_____

_____

_____

Day 18
Out to Sea

In Deuteronomy 31:8, Moses teaches, "Do not be afraid or discouraged, for the Lord will personally go ahead of you. He will be with you; he will neither fail you nor abandon you." This verse came alive for me during a very scary situation a couple of summers ago. Our family was enjoying our yearly vacation at the beach and engaging in one of our favorite activities, floating in the ocean. Before the trip, I had bought a giant new float, upon which my 8-year-old nephew, Dylan, was reclining. Although the adults were holding onto the float, the wind was particularly strong that day. So, more quickly than we could react, a powerful gust of wind caught the float and sent my nephew sailing out to sea.

Being a strong swimmer, I took off after him, but the wind was faster than me. I yelled for Dylan to jump off the float, but even wearing a life jacket, he was too afraid to disembark. So, out to sea we went—my nephew on the raft and me swimming along behind. I knew he was terrified, but I didn't want him to be terrified *and* alone. So, I kept swimming and calling out to Jesus with every stroke!

Thankfully, my sister had the sense to go to shore and recruit help, which God had already provided. Two men with canoes just happened to be right there on the shore. Without hesitation, they paddled out and towed Dylan back to shore.

Before my nephew was ever in danger, God had gone before us to orchestrate a rescue plan. As my nephew had floated out to sea, I wasn't able to see the help that God had prepared. Yet even though I couldn't see God's hand at work until the situation seemed dire, he was protecting us the entire time.

You need to know that God is doing the same thing in your life. You may not need a literal rescue from the depths of the sea, but your Father is powerful enough to protect you from whatever situation you face. Even better, he has already gone before you to put his plan of protection into action. He has a solution before you encounter the problem.

Unfortunately, we sometimes try to solve our problems on our own instead of trusting God. Can you imagine if I had declined the aid of the men in the canoes? If I had said, "No, I'll catch him eventually. I can handle this myself." The thought is ridiculous, but that's exactly how we, at times, respond to God's assistance. Instead, let's remember to put faith over fear, lean into the promises of God, and accept the protection that he offers in every area of our life.

Father, thank you for going before me and protecting me in every circumstance. Help me to accept the provision and protection you offer. Forgive me for trying to solve my problems in my own way instead of trusting in your promises. I surrender my worry, fear, and anxiety to you. Teach me to rest in your strong, capable hands, and help me grow in faith. In Jesus' name, Amen.

Personal Reflection

Prayerfully reflect on any personal problems or scary situations in your life—physical, financial, relational, professional, or anything else that is troubling your heart. Make a list below, ask God to help you navigate each with integrity, and confess your faith in his protection over you in each situation. Remember that he already knows each need, and he is working behind the scenes on your behalf.

Day 19
Words of Wisdom

Yesterday, we discussed God's hand of protection, and I shared the harrowing situation in which my nephew floated out to sea. Today, I would like to consider one of the means by which God protects us: wise counsel. But first, let me tell you about my older son Asher.

Asher was born with the demeanor of a little old man. Even as a child, he was calm and cautious, and he heartily disapproved of any rule-breaking. Now, at the age of 19, he is just as cautious and law-abiding, and is becoming quite the wise young man. In fact, he has words of wisdom to offer in just about every situation, even when no one has asked for his counsel.

So, just prior to my nephew getting blown away, Asher had offered a bit of unsolicited advice. As my sister, myself, and the younger kids floated and played in the water, Asher began making his way toward us from the shore. Yet, he wouldn't walk all the way out. He calmly said, "You guys are too deep. You need to move toward the shore." I would love to say that we heeded his advice and moved to shallower water, but you already know what happened.

Once the whole ordeal was over, Asher enjoyed a glorious "I told you so" moment, and I had no choice but to concede that we should have listened to him. His wise counsel would have averted a terrifying situation and prevented the panic that gripped every single person on the beach that day.

Scripture has much to say about listening to wise counsel. In Proverbs, we learn that the wise person heeds advice and accepts instruction (19:20), that if we do not forsake wisdom, she will protect us (4:6–7), and that learning to live wisely results in prosperity (19:8). In the New Testament, James exhorts us to ask God for wisdom, because our Father will grant our request in abundance (James 1:5).

While God might grant our request by imparting wisdom to our own heart, he sometimes provides wisdom through the words of a friend, or my teenage son. Let's learn to heed wise counsel instead of doing things our own way. Let's listen when the "Asher" in our life suggests a course change. Let's seek the guidance of the Holy Spirit and follow where he leads.

Father, thank you for making your wisdom available and generously providing wise counsel. I pray for you to grant me wisdom in abundance. Give me wisdom in my relationships, interactions, and speech. Help me heed wisdom from the trusted friends you have placed in my life, and teach me to recognize who those individuals are. Equip me to tell the difference between godly counsel and the false wisdom of the world. As I seek to heed your wisdom and live out the values of your Kingdom, empower me to inspire others to live lives filled with godly wisdom. In Jesus' name, Amen.

Personal Reflection

First, consider who God may have placed in your life to offer wise counsel. If you can't think of anyone, ask God to bring a mentor or wise friend into your life. Second, consult your list of pending decisions from Days 14 and 15. Ask God to grant you a greater measure of wisdom in each situation and consider talking through your list with your mentor or wise friend.

Day 19

Day 20
I'm Burning

The last couple of days, I described the scary situation in which my nephew floated out to sea. Because I shared a story about my nephew, I thought I would tell you about a different ordeal with my niece.

As we often do on yearly beach vacations, we rented a pontoon boat in order to spend the day exploring Saint Joseph Bay, a sea inlet filled with marine life. I'll share more about that soon, but for now, let's discuss Lilly's experience on the boat.

In her defense, Lilly was only about five years old, and the weather was hot. On top of the heat, the blazing sunshine, abrasive sand, and sticky saltwater created a combination of sensations that Lilly simply couldn't tolerate. Despite our best efforts to keep her in the shade, cooled off, and covered in sunscreen, she became increasingly irate. Eventually, Lilly planted herself in the direct sunlight, face toward the sky, and began to wail, "I'M BURNING!!!" She wouldn't cool off in the water, sit in the shade on the boat, or budge from her position in the full sun. She simply continued to wail, scream, and cry. I'm not sure how long her tantrum continued, but it seemed like an eternity before we were finally able to get her into the water and cooled off.

Although Lilly's behavior was not unusual for a young child under duress, her response highlights an important point for you and me. If we want our circumstance to change, we have to do something about it!

In Scripture, Esther embodies this principle. In the book that bears her name, the royal advisor Haman convinced King Xerxes to issue an edict to annihilate the Jews. When the edict was dispatched, Esther, the Jewish queen, took action. She gathered information, sought wise counsel, and devised a plan (Esther 3:13–4:17). She said to her uncle Mordecai, "Go and gather together all the Jews of Susa and fast for me. Do not eat or drink for three days, night or day. My maids and I will do the same. And then, though it is against the law, I will go in to see the king. If I must die, I must die," (Esther 4:16). Instead of being paralyzed by fear or surrendering to despair, Esther remained calm, sought the Lord, and did everything in her power to avert the disaster that was careening toward her people. And if you are familiar with the story, you already know that God protected his people and executed justice on their behalf.

The author of the narrative makes no explicit statement about Esther's faith. However, her words and actions reveal that she held a deep and abiding trust in her Father. Because of her faith, she had the confidence to stand up and take action on behalf of herself and her people.

Just as God equipped Esther with the resources, people, and position she needed to avert a tragic circumstance, he will provide for you. Yet, just as Esther stepped out in faith and utilized the assets God provided, our Father likewise calls us to utilize our unique blessings.

Let me close by saying that after Lilly's incident on the pontoon boat, "I'm burning" has become one of our favorite catchphrases. Although her distress wasn't humorous at the moment, we look back on the situation with laughter. Whenever things aren't going well for one of us, we wail "I'm burning" to lighten the mood, but also to remind ourselves to do something about it!

Father, thank you for providing all the resources I need to navigate life successfully. I ask you to grant me wisdom in greater measure as well as wise counselors to help me make good decisions. Teach me to take action when I am distressed instead of wallowing in self-pity or allowing myself to become incapacitated by emotional overload. I repent of complaining instead of taking meaningful action in areas of life with which I'm unsatisfied. Give me the courage to stand up and speak out when needed and the discernment to know when to remain silent. In Jesus' name, Amen.

Personal Reflection

Consider any situations in your life that are causing distress or discontentment. Write down your most difficult situation below and ask God to reveal the resources he has provided to help you solve your problem. Prayerfully determine one step you can take to move toward resolution today.

_____

_____

_____

_____

_____

_____

_____

_____

_____

Day 20

_____

_____

_____

_____

_____

_____

_____

_____

_____

_____

_____

_____

_____

_____

_____

_____

_____

Day 21
Seashells by the Seashore

Yesterday I told you about Lilly's miserable experience on the pontoon boat, so today I thought I would share a happier story. My whole family loves spending time at the beach and soaking in the beauty of God's creation. Lilly and I especially enjoy wading through the surf looking for seashells. Being the type-A perfectionist that I am, I always look for shells with no chips, cracks, or flaws.

One particular year, we had an abundance of shells from which to choose. Despite the abundance of pristine, undamaged shells. Lilly, however, kept choosing broken ones. At first, I thought she was choosing shells at random, but then I realized she was choosing them especially for their flaws. As she held a chipped and broken shell in her hands, she declared, "Isn't it beautiful?" I looked at her treasure, and realized that the broken areas created unique swirls, spirals, and shapes. Examined through a different lens, the seashell truly was beautiful.

Admiring the broken seashell prompted me to meditate on my own flaws. Although I am an imperfect creature, my Father calls me a "masterpiece" (Ephesians 2:10). Further, Paul teaches that our weaknesses, in God's hands, become strengths. When the apostle begged God to take away his infirmity, "[God] said, 'My grace is all you need. My power works best in weakness.' So now I am glad to boast about my weaknesses, so that the power of Christ can work through me. That's why I take pleasure in my weaknesses, and in the insults, hardships, persecutions, and troubles that I suffer for Christ. For when I am weak, then I am strong," (2 Corinthians 12:9–10).

God sometimes allows brokenness in our lives. Of course, the process of being broken isn't something we enjoy, but the result creates something more beautiful than before. As trials chip away at our pride, selfishness, and self-sufficiency, we learn to rely on our Father and sustain ourselves on his strength.

As a matter of fact, the ultimate act of brokenness brought the ultimate healing to our world. When Jesus died on the cross, he suffered horribly, but through his death and resurrection he made it possible for us to be healed from every trial, illness, and distress. Just like the broken seashells, God is creating something beautiful and unique through your weakness or struggle. Let's let those fractured parts of our life become something beautiful.

Father, thank you for making me strong even when I am weak. Help me see the beauty in the broken parts of my life and character. I repent of doubting you and becoming angry when my life doesn't go as planned. As I submit my flaws to you, I ask you to transform them for your glory. Give me a greater measure of persistence and resilience so that I'm not tempted to give up as I'm being continually molded into your masterpiece. In Jesus' name, Amen.

Personal Reflection

Think of a time in your past when God transformed one of your weaknesses into something beautiful. Then prayerfully meditate on how he might use your current struggle for your benefit and his glory. If you aren't sure, pray for him to grow your faith enough to trust him through the trial.

Day 22
Seahorses & Seaweed

One of the activities we enjoy on our yearly beach trip is searching for sea creatures. We even have a competition over who can find the most interesting creature. In the summer of 2021, I declared myself the clear winner. As I was wading in water up to my chest, I found a seahorse in a small patch of seaweed—my first live seahorse! I was overjoyed by my discovery.

Then, because I knew where to look, I continued to find seahorse after seahorse. Apparently, the lovely creatures like to camouflage themselves in clumps of seaweed. Their shape and color blends in perfectly. That such a beautiful little creature would be hidden in something so mundane seemed bizarre to me. I began to ask myself what other wonderful things I might be missing because they are masked by the mundane.

The authors of Scripture teach us that God has an abundant store of good things for those who love him. According to Psalm 31:19–20:

> *How great is the goodness*
> *you have stored up for those who fear you.*
> *You lavish it on those who come to you for protection,*
> *blessing them before the watching world.*
> *You hide them in the shelter of your presence,*
> *safe from those who conspire against them.*
> *You shelter them in your presence,*
> *far from accusing tongues.*
> **Psalm 31:19–20**

Our Father isn't stingy or miserly. He loves to bless his children and he does so all the time. Yet sometimes we don't notice his blessings because they come in the midst of the mundane. For example, if we have a roof over our heads and food in our pantry, we are blessed!

Sometimes God blesses us by hiding us away from the trials of life or the schemes of the Enemy. Life might seem uneventful and boring because God is shielding us from conflict or persecution. In those seasons, we typically don't even realize our Father is protecting and blessing us. When we only watch for the big, dramatic blessings, we fail to enjoy the multitude of daily blessings he lavishes upon us.

Acknowledging our blessings can impact our entire outlook on life. When we are diligent to acknowledge our blessings and express gratitude, we are constantly aware of his love, protection, and affection. Such a mindset simply doesn't leave much room for worry or complaining. Let's remember to look for those seahorses in the seaweed today!

Father, I am eternally thankful for your love and care. Open my eyes to the blessings by which I'm surrounded, big and small. Help me see your hand of goodness even in the midst of the mundane. Thank you most of all for blessing me with forgiveness and salvation. Help me to, in turn, be a blessing to others. In Jesus' name, Amen.

Personal Reflection

Be intentional to look for blessings in the midst of the mundane today!

_____

_____

_____

Day 22

Day 23
Sea Urchins

One hazard of our aquatic explorations in Saint Joseph Bay are the sea urchins. Urchins are echinoderms, the class of marine invertebrate that also includes starfish and sand dollars. Unlike their harmless cousins, however, urchins are covered in venomous spines. The venom is rarely fatal, but stepping on an urchin is quite painful. And urchins are all over Saint Joseph Bay. In fact, stepping on one is a near certainty. Therefore, each person in the family is careful to wear water shoes as we explore the area.

Nonetheless, on one particular day as we began exploring, my mom excitedly hopped out of our pontoon boat, feet-first, with no shoes. And she landed right on an urchin. She immediately hopped back into the boat to extract the barbed spines from her foot, which can cause infection if not removed. Needless to say, the damaged foot remained painful, red, and swollen for the remainder of our week at the beach.

The urchins make me think of the trials of life. We know they will occur, yet we fail to remain on guard and take precautions. We feel surprised when we face painful losses, stinging betrayals, and venomous words. We get angry with God, when in fact, he has already told us exactly what to expect. In John 16:33b, shortly before his crucifixion, Jesus sought to fortify the faith of his disciples, saying, "Here on earth you will have many trials and sorrows. But take heart, because I have overcome the world." Our Savior suffered greatly throughout his life, facing betrayal, rejection, mockery, torture, and death. In doing so, he took the punishment we deserve, but he also modeled a life of faith in a fallen world. In taking up our own crosses to follow him, we should expect to face trials, though hopefully none as extreme as those faced by our Lord. Nonetheless, we should expect loss, betrayal, rejection, and pain. We know those spiky little urchins are lurking in the waters of life. Instead of being shocked each time we encounter one, we can take preemptive steps to minimize damage. We can also fortify our faith in the knowledge that we are walking in the footsteps of our Savior. Our suffering isn't a surprise to him, nor should it be to us. Instead of doubting him in times of trial, lets learn to walk more closely by his side.

Jesus, thank you for modeling a life of faith and obedience in the face of suffering. Teach me to walk in your footsteps and bear my own cross with fortitude. Give me wisdom to take steps that will protect my heart, faith, and family. I repent of blaming you and doubting you during painful seasons of life. Train me to trust you more during trials rather than pulling away. Empower me to learn and grow as I persevere through each difficult situation I face. In Jesus' name. Amen.

Personal Reflection

What steps can you take to protect your heart and fortify your faith in the face of future trials. Perhaps you need to set relational or emotional boundaries. Perhaps you need to be more faithful in your spiritual disciplines like prayer and Bible study. Perhaps you need to foster a mindset of gratitude and joy. You might also think back to seasons of trial in your past. What helped you move forward, heal, and maybe even grow in faith? Prayerfully meditate, then write 2–3 action steps below.

Day 24
Fallen Star

A sea creature that we often encounter during our summer beach explorations is the starfish. The first time we encountered one of the fascinating creatures, we learned that starfish, like lizards, utilize autotomy as a defense mechanism.

My younger son, Abel, was the first to discover a starfish resting on the ocean floor. He gently lifted the creature out of the water so that we could all admire it. Within seconds, everyone gasped in horror as the legs of the starfish began falling off. Abel immediately dropped all the pieces back into the water, hoping the starfish hadn't harmed itself permanently.

For a long time, the thought of that starfish made me sad. I worried that we had harmed an innocent creature. When I finally did a bit of research, however, I realized that the little star was perfectly fine. Actually, he was better than fine. I learned that starfish have a rare ability to regenerate an entire body from each piece. Although the growth process can take up to a year, each severed limb absorbs nutrients from its environment and re-grows essential organs.

The process of autotomy and regeneration is similar to the principal Jesus teaches in John 12:24-25, "I tell you the truth, unless a kernel of wheat is planted in the soil and dies, it remains alone. But its death will produce many new kernels—a plentiful harvest of new lives." Like the starfish, we must sever certain aspects of our own lives so that other parts can experience spiritual birth. We are called to prune not only sins, but also preferences, conveniences, and personal desires. I'm not saying that God wants us to sacrifice every comfort, but the more we sacrifice our own wants, the more space we create to help others find life in Christ. What limbs might you need to amputate from your life today?

Jesus, thank you for giving your own life so that I could be born as a new creation. Teach me to sacrifice my own desires and preferences so that I can help others experience your grace. Reveal which areas of my life might need to be cut away in order to make space for me to more effectively spread the Gospel. Fill my heart with such love for you and your people that I consider my own wants of no consequence compared to the blessing of serving you. In Jesus' name, Amen.

Personal Reflection

Be creative and imagine yourself as a starfish. Imagine that the various aspects of your life are limbs extending from your center. Consider what your limbs are composed of (family, hobbies, profession, dreams, desires, habits, thoughts, patterns of behavior). Make a list below, or if you feel creative, draw your starfish. Once you're finished, ask God to reveal any limbs that might need to be removed so that you are better equipped to serve him.

_____

_____

_____

_____

_____

Day 24

Day 25
Sneaky Stingrays

Another sea creature we encounter frequently on our beach adventures is the stingray. Although the creatures are quite dangerous, I find them strikingly beautiful. They are also strikingly hard to spot. Unless they are in motion, the lithe rays blend in perfectly with the sandy ocean floor. They are so well camouflaged that humans are encouraged to shuffle their feet when walking in the ocean.

In the area we most frequently explore, rays (and other sea creatures) are plentiful. Thus, my family wears water shoes *and* shuffles our feet. Thanks to taking precautions, I narrowly missed stepping on a ray last year. As I shuffled my feet, a large stingray seemed to leap from the ocean floor and zoom away at an astonishing speed. I was delighted to have come so close to one of my favorite creatures, but also relieved not to have stepped on it—for his sake and my own.

I was also astonished that a stingray could be so close at hand (or foot) while I was completely unaware. As I thought about the rays, which are always present in the ocean yet typically unseen, I meditated on the presence of God. Our Father is always with us, even when we aren't conscious of his presence. God says through the prophet Isaiah,

> *Do not fear, for I have redeemed you;*
> *I have summoned you by name; you are mine.*
> *When you pass through the waters,*

I will be with you;
and when you pass through the rivers,
they will not sweep over you.
When you walk through the fire,
you will not be burned;
the flames will not set you ablaze.
For I am the Lord your God,
the Holy One of Israel, your Savior;
Isaiah 43:1a-3a

No matter where we are or where we go, God is with us. No matter whether we acknowledge his presence or even want him near, our Father is by our side. He carries us, guards us, and protects us from harm. In the light of his constant presence, we can navigate life with confidence and joy.

When the deep waters of our trials threaten to sweep us away, we can remain anchored in his care. When the fires of adversity burn hot, we can remain cool in his peace. Even when we don't see him or feel him, we can take heart because the Creator of the universe is by our side.

Father, thank you for continually remaining by my side and in my heart. When I am tempted to fret or fear, help me remember that you are with me. Give me a greater awareness of your presence and a greater confidence in your protection. Empower me to overcome every worry and trial through the joy that comes from abiding in you. Forgive me for ignoring you and taking you for granted. Teach me to walk with you as a dear friend and constant companion. In Jesus' name, Amen.

Personal Reflection

Seek to cultivate a greater awareness of God's presence today. Set an hourly reminder on your watch or phone to acknowledge God, pray for any needs that might arise, and thank him for his presence.

_____

_____

_____

_____

_____

_____

_____

_____

_____

_____

_____

_____

_____

_____

Day 26
Whatever Floats Your Boat

As I mentioned a few days ago, my family often rents a pontoon boat to explore Saint Joseph Bay during our Florida vacations. Once out on the water, we make frequent stops during which we hop out of the boat and explore the aquatic terrain. Each time we "park," we deploy the boat's anchor into the water. The anchor is an absolute necessity, as without it, the boat would float away and leave us stranded. Even if the weather is pleasant and the seas are calm, ocean currents will cause the boat to drift. Yet, if our anchor is firmly grounded, we can enjoy our explorations without worry or fear.

In Scripture, our faith in God is similarly described as an anchor. According to Hebrews 6:19, "This hope is a strong and trustworthy anchor for our souls. It leads us through the curtain into God's inner sanctuary." In other words, our faith anchors our lives and enables us to abide in the very presence of God. When we cultivate a lifestyle of trust in God, we won't drift from his truth or walk away from his presence. Conversely, if we allow ourselves to doubt his promises, plans, or purposes, we begin to drift further and further away.

Don't get me wrong, we all have occasional moments of doubt. Yet, we can choose to remain anchored in Christ by replacing the doubt with the truth of God's promises in Scripture. Furthermore, remaining anchored in our faith and abiding in God's presence isn't always an emotional experience. The whole point of being anchored in him is that even in moments (or days or weeks or months) that we don't *feel* his presence, we don't drift out to sea and drown.

So, how firmly anchored is your faith today? Are you drifting toward deep and dangerous waters of uncertainty? Or are you so secure that you can live your life and explore the terrain without worry or fear? Let's drop anchor and relax in his presence today.

Jesus, thank you for providing a secure foundation in which I can anchor my life. Thank you for making a way for me to enter into the presence of God and empowering me to abide in your love. I ask you to expose any tendrils of doubt in my heart so that I can replace them with the truth of your Word. Forgive me for doubting your goodness, provision, and protection. Help me grow into a more mature faith that doesn't rely on emotional experiences or external affirmations. In Jesus' name, Amen.

Personal Reflection

Prayerfully examine your heart and ask God to reveal any areas of life in which you are doubting his goodness or faithfulness. Make a list below and then find a Scripture verse for each in order to replace your doubt with the truth of God's Word. Come back and read them every day until your doubts begin to abate.

Day 26

_____

_____

_____

_____

_____

_____

_____

_____

_____

_____

_____

_____

_____

_____

_____

_____

Day 27
Seasick

In a spring devotional, I shared about learning to fish with my Pops and graduating to deep sea fishing trips when I was older. During my teenage and young adult years, our family would charter a boat each year during our Florida vacation and spend the day fishing miles out in the Gulf. Once I had babies, taking a whole day to go deep sea fishing simply wasn't an option. Thus, I took a roughly 10-year hiatus until the boys were old enough to come along.

The first year back on a deep-sea fishing trip, I was ecstatic. As we boarded our boat and headed toward deep water, I relished the cool wind in my face and the soft morning sun on my skin. The water was a bit choppy, but not severe enough to deter serious fishermen (and fisherwomen).

The trip to deep water takes close to an hour, so we all reclined on the front of the boat to enjoy the ride. As the minutes passed, my joy slowly transitioned to discomfort as the choppy sea made my stomach roil. I'd never in my life become seasick, but apparently bearing children had altered my constitution. I was soon hanging over the side of the boat sharing my breakfast with the fish. I would like to say that I felt better after emptying my stomach, but I didn't. However, I wasn't willing to miss the opportunity to fish. So I proceeded to alternate between fishing and retching all day long.

Like my fraught day upon the choppy sea, life sometimes throws us off balance and turns joyful expectations into a nauseating mess.

But the good news is that although life can make us seasick, Jesus can calm the storm. Matthew records,

> *Then Jesus got into the boat and started across the lake with his disciples. Suddenly, a fierce storm struck the lake, with waves breaking into the boat. But Jesus was sleeping. The disciples went and woke him up, shouting, "Lord, save us! We're going to drown!" Jesus responded, "Why are you afraid? You have so little faith!" Then he got up and rebuked the wind and waves, and suddenly there was a great calm. The disciples were amazed. "Who is this man?" they asked. "Even the winds and waves obey him!"*
>
> ### Matthew 8:23–27

We serve a God who is master of the wind and waves. Even better, he is the master of our lives. Although our circumstances may become precarious or unsettling, he can bring calm to the storm.

Sometimes our Lord brings peace by calming the storm that rages around us, and sometimes he calms the storm in our hearts. Either way, no tempest is strong enough to throw our Lord off balance. We only have to trust in his strength and stay in the boat with him. In plain terms, we stay faithful, walk in his ways, and remain obedient even when we are tempted to seek our own solutions through worldly means. When we trust God to calm the wind and waves, our spirits feel better than my stomach on prescription strength Dramamine.

Jesus, thank you for calling me into the boat with you and calming the storms of life. I repent of stepping out of the boat and trying to solve problems my own way instead of trusting you. I ask you to calm the turmoil in my heart and bring resolution to the difficult situations in my life. Help me walk in greater faith and obedience each day. As I learn to trust you in greater measure, grant me joy that can't be diminished by any circumstance. In Jesus' name, Amen.

Personal Reflection

Make a list of any disappointments or difficult situations you are navigating, and pray over each item in your list. Ask God to bring peace to your heart and resolution in each circumstance. Then ask him how you can walk in greater obedience and faith through each.

_____

_____

_____

_____

_____

_____

_____

_____

_____

_____

_____

_____

Day 28
Jellyfish Stings

A common hazard of swimming in the ocean is jellyfish. From year to year, we never know what to expect. Some years, the surf will be clear of all stinging menaces, some years the water will be positively brimming with gelatinous creatures, but most years, the jellyfish content of the ocean is somewhere in between.

A few years back, we encountered a moderate concentration of jellyfish on our beach vacation. As usual, we avoided the stinging goo without paying the creatures much attention. However, Abel, who tends to leap before he looks, managed to get the long tentacles of a large jellyfish wrapped entirely around his arm. We quickly extricated his limb and exited the water, but the damage had been done. His entire upper arm looked burned, and he assured us that the sting was quite painful. Thankfully, Abel has a very high pain tolerance, and with a little cortisone cream continued to enjoy the beach. He ventured right back into the ocean without hesitation. One little—or large—jellyfish wasn't going to steal his joy or prevent him from enjoying his favorite place, the ocean.

Abel's response to the jellyfish made me ponder my own response to things and people who hurt me. In the past, when I've endured serious emotional wounds, my response is to withdraw. I pull away from everyone, not just the ones who hurt me. I retreat into my safe space of relational isolation and emotional segregation.

Yet, detachment is precisely the opposite of the manner in which our Father calls us to respond to pain. When we isolate ourselves from the people God places in our lives, we cut off avenues of healing. Even worse, as we grow increasingly distant from our friends, family and faith, we grow increasingly distant from our Father.

Jude discusses the manner in which believers should respond to relational strife and emotional pain. In his short letter, he cautions us about ungodly people who harm God's people, even infiltrating the church and hurting believers from within. Rather than turning from the church, Jude exhorts God's people to encourage one another. He teaches,

> *But you, dear friends, must build each other up in your most holy faith, pray in the power of the Holy Spirit, and await the mercy of our Lord Jesus Christ, who will bring you eternal life. In this way, you will keep yourselves safe in God's love. And you must show mercy to those whose faith is wavering. Rescue others by snatching them from the flames of judgment. Show mercy to still others, but do so with great caution, hating the sins that contaminate their lives. Now all glory to God, who is able to keep you from falling away and will bring you with great joy into his glorious presence without a single fault.*

Jude 1:20–24

Perhaps you were hurt by someone in the church; perhaps by someone in your family; perhaps by a friend or colleague. Whatever the situation, our Lord calls us to lean into our faith family. As we encourage others, we are likewise encouraged. As we pray for others, we receive prayer. As we show mercy, we receive mercy. As we continue to abide in the love of Christ and the family of faith, we begin to heal, and one day before we know it, we'll be once more full of joy.

Father, thank you for working to bring healing and wholeness in my life. Show me the people to whom you would have me turn when my heart is broken. Forgive me for withdrawing from my faith family when I am hurting. Teach me to continue walking in love, mercy, and grace even when I'm dealing with emotional wounds. I ask you to increase my perseverance as I navigate trials, grow my faith, and restore my joy. In Jesus' name, Amen.

Personal Reflection

Prayerfully consider whether you are harboring any unhealed hurts in your heart. Make a point to talk with a friend or mentor this week to talk and pray over your wounds. Also be sure to share a few words of encouragement as well!

_____

_____

_____

_____

_____

_____

_____

_____

_____

Day 29
Fearless Faith

Over the last couple of weeks, we've discussed both delightful and harrowing beach memories. Today, I'd like to jump from the seashores of the Gulf of Mexico back to sweet home Alabama.

When I was a child, I lived on a farm in the country, and I was in heaven. I spent my days playing in the fields and forests and only came home at the end of the day to eat, sleep, and repeat. Most of the fields were bounded by barbed wire to keep various farm animals penned in. The fences weren't a problem for me because, as a little girl, I was small enough to slip between the rows of wire. Yet, on one particular day, the barbed wire fencing became a very big problem. Then, just as now, I had long, thick, messy hair. When my hair came into contact with the barbed wire, I got stuck—completely stuck. I couldn't go back, I couldn't go forward, and I could not get my hair untangled.

Since I wasn't terribly far from the house, and I have a very loud voice, I simply started yelling for my mom. I wasn't afraid because I knew my mom would hear me. I was annoyed and uncomfortable, but I knew she would come and help. And, of course, she did.

What if we responded to every frightening situation in life with faith in our Father? In Isaiah 41:13, God says, "For I am the Lord your God, who takes hold of your right hand and says to you, Do not fear; I will help you." Often, when we face difficult situations or encounter unexpected trials, our default setting is fear. But we can learn to flip that response. Instead of freaking out, we can simply call out to our

Heavenly Father and wait expectantly for His help. The waiting might be uncomfortable, just as when I was snared in the fence, but if we stay calm, the discomfort won't morph into all-out panic.

Allow me to point out that my mom didn't come and rescue me right away. She heard the sound of my shouting, but she initially thought it was the goats making noise. I had to wait a little while, but I continued calling out for help because I knew she would come.

Our Heavenly Father knows every hair on our heads, and he knows when we are snagged in a difficult situation. If it seems that he isn't responding as quickly as we expect or in the manner we expect, he might be working in the background in ways we don't see. Or he might just be working *in* us, refining and untangling our souls. Instead of reverting to fear, let's continue calling out in faith, and wait expectantly for his aid to arrive at just the right moment.

Father, I confess that my default response to trials is often fear. Forgive me for failing to trust in your power and love. Thank you for watching over me in every moment of my life and working in my heart. Teach me to trust you more and grow my faith. I ask you to cause my fear to wither away so that my first instinct is to call out to you. Help me take captive any fearful thoughts and submit them to the truth of your Word. Thank you for guiding me, strengthening me, and rescuing me from every snare that comes my way. In Jesus' name, Amen.

Personal Reflection

Prayerfully consider how you have responded to any fearful or difficult situations in your past. What can you learn from your response, and how can you respond with more faith in the future? Write your thoughts below.

Day 30
Thermodynamics

When I became a follower of Christ, I knew little about the Bible. I understood the basics—that Jesus had died on the Cross so that my sins could be forgiven and that I would get to spend eternity in "Heaven" instead of going to "Hell" when I died. Beyond that, my knowledge of my new faith was pretty sparse.

Let me explain this way. My undergraduate degree is in chemical engineering, and one of the hardest courses in the program was chemical engineering thermodynamics. ChemE Thermo was widely known as the course that would separate the men from the boys, or in my case, the women from the girls. It was also the course that compelled many chemical engineering students to switch to a different branch of engineering.

When I began the course, I understood some of the terminology, and I could talk about the subject on a surface level. I knew that thermodynamics involved changes in energy and material properties. However, I didn't understand exactly what those changes were and the processes by which they took place. As I progressed through the course, I began to understand the subject at a deeper level. I could balance complex chemical equations and describe the effects of the reactions. Basically, I learned what happens, how it happens, and why it happens.

Not to brag, but I passed the course with flying colors. Soon after, I accepted a paid internship in the industry and used what I'd learned to manage and improve actual chemical processes. In a literal way, I was creating change in the physical world around me.

My journey with Jesus progressed in a similar manner. When I accepted Jesus as Lord and "got saved," I learned that I was supposed to share my new faith and "witness" to others, which was far more frightening than chemical engineering thermodynamics. Because I didn't really understand the depth and significance of what had happened in my heart, I wanted more time to learn before I tried to explain it to others. So, I took time to study the Bible and spent time with God in prayer.

As my understanding grew, I realized that having a relationship with Jesus isn't just about getting to heaven when I die. When I accepted Jesus, he began transforming my life, inside and out—not just in the future when I die, but right now. Jesus' life-changing work is described in Matthew 9:35, "Jesus traveled through all the towns and villages of that area, teaching in the synagogues and announcing the Good News about the Kingdom. And he healed every kind of disease and illness. When he saw the crowds, he had compassion on them because they were confused and helpless, like sheep without a shepherd," (Matthew 9: 35–36).

Jesus traveled the region sharing the Good News, healing the sick, and ministering to those who were "confused and helpless," or translated alternately as "weary and worn out." Jesus' ministry to the confused, helpless, weary and worn-out continues today! When we accept Jesus, he cares for us and becomes part of our lives. Through his work in our life, our whole existence changes for the better.

Then, just as I used my knowledge of chemical processes to effect change, we get to use our knowledge of our Savior to create change in other people. We get to share the wonderful news about a savior who heals, helps, and changes us right here and now! And an encounter with Jesus creates change more profound and lasting than any chemical reaction.

Jesus, thank you for making a way for me to have a life-giving relationship with my Heavenly Father. Thank you for filling my life with purpose and joy, in both peaceful seasons and challenging times. I ask today that you would open my eyes to people who don't know you, especially those within my own family and circle of influence. Allow me to see people through your eyes, and like you, have such great compassion that I am moved to action. Give me the courage and the words to speak on your behalf. Help me also live a life of integrity that speaks more loudly than my words and causes others to desire a relationship with you. I ask that you would prepare hearts in advance to accept your invitation to receive new life. Thank you for going before me to prepare the way. In Jesus' Name, Amen.

Personal Reflection

Prayerfully meditate on your own process of growth in Christ. Are you continuing to grow and transform? As you grow in your understanding of God and his Word, how might your Father be calling you to share the transformative power of Christ?

_____

_____

_____

_____

_____

_____

Day 31
Practice Makes Progress

Yesterday we discussed the process of learning and growing in Christ. Sometimes, however, we seem to be spinning our wheels. Growth seems non-existent, and our faith feels lifeless. However, faith shouldn't be rooted in how we feel or dependent upon emotional highs. A lasting walk with God requires perseverance.

Paul teaches that our Father will never stop working in our lives. He exhorts,

> *And I am certain that God, who began the good work within you, will continue his work until it is finally finished on the day when Christ Jesus returns. . . . I pray that your love will overflow more and more, and that you will keep on growing in knowledge and understanding. For I want you to understand what really matters, so that you may live pure and blameless lives until the day of Christ's return. May you always be filled with the fruit of your salvation—the righteous character produced in your life by Jesus Christ—for this will bring much glory and praise to God.*
>
> ### *Philippians 1:6, 9–11*

Paul calls us to partner with God, continuously seeking to grow in love, knowledge, and understanding. He encourages us to live a pure and blameless life, and to be filled with righteous character.

Sure, Paul, I'll get right on that. Honestly, I can't say that I fulfill every one of those qualifications, even on my best day. But Paul isn't being legalistic or judgmental. He is describing the *ideal* that we should be working toward.

Allow me to illustrate. Growing in spiritual maturity is sort of like working out to get in better shape. When I was about 9 years old, I started doing aerobics with my mom. It was the Jane Fonda era, and the heyday of aerobics, complete with leotards and leg warmers. I remember that during my very first class, I thought I was going to die. I was gasping for air, every muscle in my body was burning, and I was thirsty beyond belief. (Back then, no one had water bottles. We had to get a quick, slurping drink at the communal water fountain when the instructor gave us a break.) The experience was so harrowing that I wasn't sure I ever wanted to do it again. But I like a good challenge, so I went back again . . . and again . . . and again. My progress was so slow that I didn't even realize change was happening until a friend commented that my "butt was shrinking." Although my goal hadn't been weight-loss, my body had begun to lose fat and grow stronger. I also realized, at that moment, that more had changed than my physical appearance. The classes were no longer traumatic—I had started to enjoy them.

As time passed, my love for fitness grew so much that I became a fitness instructor and personal trainer in my twenties. Now, in my forties, I still love fitness. I can't do high-impact aerobics like I did back in the Jane Fonda days, but I'm an avid cyclist and I'm faster than I've ever been.

My point is that our walk with God is about perseverance. If we love God, we will strive to become a better Jesus follower throughout our lives. We may not make gains every day, but as long as we persevere, we'll continue making forward progress. Just like working out, the progress might be slow to the point of barely noticeable, but over the course of weeks, months, and years, the change in our heart and the change in our character will be astounding. As we close, let's pray Paul's words over our own lives:

Father, I am certain that you will continue your work in me until it is finally finished on the day when Christ Jesus returns. I pray that my love for you and your people will overflow more and more, and that I will continue growing in knowledge and understanding. Help me perceive what really matters, so that I can live pure and blameless until the day of Christ's return. May I always be filled with the fruit of my salvation—the righteous character produced in my life by Jesus Christ. I pray that my life will bring much glory and praise to you, my Father, my Lord, and my Savior. In Jesus' name, Amen.

Personal Reflection

Prayerfully reflect on your capacity for perseverance in dry seasons. Do you maintain healthy spiritual habits, such as prayer, Bible study, and worship? Or do you wait for an emotional experience to rekindle your devotion? Ask God to help you honestly assess your growth trajectory. Determine at least one strategy for maintaining greater perseverance in your walk with Christ, and write it below.

_____

_____

_____

_____

_____

_____

_____

_____

_____

_____

_____

_____

_____

_____

_____

_____

_____

_____

_____

_____

_____

_____

_____

_____

_____

_____

Day 32
Father's Day

Since we are in proximity to Father's Day, I would like to discuss the concept of manhood. Contrary to popular opinion, masculinity is not toxic, and testosterone is not a toxin. God created men and women with different traits, roles, and temperaments. Our differences complement each other and make us stronger, while trying to homogenize our roles actually weakens the foundation of our families.

Simply being different doesn't mean one set of traits are better or worse than the other. Look at the animal world, for example. We don't chastise male lions for protecting their family from predators or female lions for hunting prey. Their roles complement each other, and we would be foolish to try to "fix" their arrangement in order to make it more egalitarian.

Another example, red foxes are excellent fathers. After the vixen gives birth, the male hunts and provides for the young for about three months. The mother fox remains with the young to nurse and protect them, remaining inside the den until the pups are ready to experience the outside world. Once the pups are able to venture outside the den, daddy will bury food nearby and teach his offspring to hunt for themselves. The doting dads also spend a great deal of time playing with their pups. Their play reveals overt affection, but also serves another function—the pretend attacks and ambushes teaches the cubs to evade and defend against predators.

Not all animals are good parents, but among species that care well for their young, we often see a beautiful symbiosis between the different roles played by the male and female. It grieves my heart to see our culture increasingly devaluing masculinity in humans. In Scripture, both masculine and feminine attributes are praised.

Since we are discussing manhood, I'd like to draw your attention to two passages. First, Paul exhorts Timothy to live as a godly man. He says, "You, Timothy, are a man of God; so run from all these evil things. Pursue righteousness and a godly life, along with faith, love, perseverance, and gentleness. Fight the good fight for the true faith. Hold tightly to the eternal life to which God has called you, which you have declared so well before many witnesses," (1 Timothy 6:11–12). Paul teaches that a man of God resists evil and pursues righteousness. A man of God exhibits faith, love, perseverance, and gentleness, while also fighting for the faith. In other words, a godly man is humble enough to be gentle and loving, but strong enough to stand his ground. In another passage, Paul speaks more specifically to husbands, exhorting men to love their wives "as Christ loved the church," (Ephesians 5:25). Just as Jesus sacrificed himself, a husband should love his wife sacrificially. Yet, just as Christ boldly took a stand against evil and led his people in righteousness, so also should a man lead his family with integrity and strength. Females have no reason to be threatened by any of these attributes. Rather, we should celebrate and encourage men in their God-given strengths.

Jesus, thank you for modeling godly manhood during your time on this earth. Help me to value and encourage the men in my life. Give our culture the wisdom to understand the value in masculinity. I pray that you would help the men in my family, community, and country find a healthy balance between strength and gentleness. Help me to hone the traits and strengths you've given me to serve and support those I love. In your name, Amen.

Personal Reflection

Reach out to a father, father-figure, or male mentor who has impacted your life and thank him today.

_____

_____

_____

_____

_____

_____

_____

_____

_____

_____

_____

_____

_____

_____

_____

Day 33
The Theory of Everything

In each volume of the *Rooted & Flourishing* series, I like to spend a few days discussing our experience of God through his creation. Today, I'd like to talk specifically about the relationship between faith and science.

I think we would all agree that the beauty and complexity of the natural world can draw us into a more profound experience of the Creator. So, does it matter whether we believe the earth evolved over billions of years or whether it was created in 7 days? Does it matter whether we endorse young-earth creationism or evolutionary biological processes? Does it matter whether we think science and faith are irreconcilable? My answer is a resounding YES, it matters! According to Psalm 19:

> *The heavens proclaim the glory of God.*
> *The skies display his craftsmanship.*
> *Day after day they continue to speak;*
> *night after night they make him known.*
> *They speak without a sound or word;*
> *their voice is never heard.*
> *Yet their message has gone throughout the earth,*
> *and their words to all the world.*
> ### *Psalm 19:1–4*

When we learn more about creation, we learn more about the Creator.

Let's start with the basics and discuss why we can confidently say that religion and science aren't at odds with one another. In short, the Bible is not a scientific textbook. To understand properly any work of literature, we must consider the intention of the author. For example, a grocery list, personal letter, and an instruction manual will be read and understood very differently. If I read a grocery list like an instruction manual or a personal letter, I'm going to be very confused! Thus, when we read Scripture like a science textbook, we come away with some misguided ideas. The Bible was written and inspired to tell us about the character of God and his relationship with his people, not to teach scientific principles.

Some interpretations of the Bible are portrayed as the only faithful way of understanding certain passages,

In passages where Scripture and science seem to contradict each other, fundamentalist teachings are often portrayed as the only faithful interpretation. Such a position is misguided at best and harmful to the spread of the Gospel at worst. For example, fundamentalists promote a literal 7-day creation as the *only* correct interpretation of Genesis 1–2. Many adherents go so far as to portray people who hold alternate views as heretical. Sadly, this attitude ostracizes many faithful believers and alienates scientifically-minded individuals.

I'll be transparent and tell you that I'm an adherent of evolutionary biological processes. However, my purpose is not to convince you that a certain interpretation is the "right" interpretation. As pastor-scholar-apologist Tim Keller says, "Genesis 1 does not teach that God made the world in six twenty-four-hour days. Of course, it doesn't teach evolution either, because it doesn't address the actual processes by which God created human life." My hope is that you will open your heart to the possibility that science actually draws us closer to the Creator, and that scientific advances are not a threat to our faith.

Father, thank you for creating the complex and beautiful world in which we live. Help me to examine my own beliefs about the interface of faith and science. Teach me to read and interpret your Word as the original authors' intended. I pray that I would have the courage to examine my beliefs about Scripture and seek your truth above all. Teach me to dialogue productively with those who hold different beliefs. In Jesus' name, Amen.

Personal Reflection

Consider your own attitude toward the intersection of faith and science. Do you immediately reject scientific theories that seem to conflict with certain interpretations of the Bible? Do you avoid the subject altogether and remain blissfully unaware? Do you seek to gain a greater understanding about how scientific discoveries can complement our beliefs and bolster our faith? Do you want to learn more, but simply aren't sure where to turn for trustworthy information? Write your thoughts below and we'll return to the subject tomorrow.

_____

_____

_____

_____

_____

_____

_____

Day 33

Day 34
Stand in Awe

Yesterday we discussed the compatibility of faith and science. We need not be afraid to scrutinize God, his Word, or his creation. The work of our Father is robust enough to withstand scrutiny. In fact, learning more about the wonders of the natural world and the vast magnitude of space draws us into a more profound experience of worship toward God.

As we discussed yesterday, the Bible was written and inspired to tell us about our Father, his character, and our relationship with him. Consider Psalm 33:

He loves whatever is just and good;
the unfailing love of the Lord fills the earth.
The Lord merely spoke,
and the heavens were created.
He breathed the word,
and all the stars were born.
He assigned the sea its boundaries
and locked the oceans in vast reservoirs.
Let the whole world fear the Lord,
and let everyone stand in awe of him.
For when he spoke, the world began!
It appeared at his command.
Psalm 33:5—9

God created the natural world in a manner that, through it, we can perceive his awesome power and goodness. According to Christian astrophysicist Jennifer J. Wiseman, "Since God is responsible for all nature, there is nothing to fear in studying the details; in fact God calls us to study his handiwork as a means to learning of God's character and glory." So, when we encounter a scientific theory that seems to contradict Scripture, we should examine both more closely, rather than simply concluding that they aren't compatible. In doing so we grow in faith, honor our Father, and draw closer to him.

Father, thank you for revealing your love, power, and goodness through your creation. Give me the wisdom to understand both your Word and your world. I repent of being lax about learning how you speak to your people through the complexities of science. Help me grow in both knowledge and faith. As I learn more about your world, teach me more about myself and my relationship with you. In Jesus' name, Amen.

Personal Reflection

Our reflection for today is a bit different than usual. I encourage you to visit Biologos.org and explore the variety of resources on the intersection of faith and science. Choose at least one article to read. If you aren't sure where to start, begin with the article I've cited in the footnote. (Scan the QR code to read the article.)

Scan the QR code for passages of Scripture or Link

Day 35
Bless Your Heart

As I began writing the Rooted and Flourishing devotional series, one of my goals was to offer at least one devotional from every book of Scripture. For the most part, fulfilling this objective wasn't too difficult. Only a couple of books presented a challenge, such as 1 Chronicles, which is virtually 29 chapters of genealogy. Although genealogies can, believe it or not, be fascinating, they aren't easy source material for devotional writing.

So, as I read through the book seeking inspiration and guidance from the Holy Spirit, nothing seemed to resonate. I didn't perceive the Lord leading me to write about anything in 1 Chronicles until I reached the very last chapter of the book. Persevering through the dense material and waiting upon God to speak, I think, could be a devotional in itself. However, that wasn't the message the Lord gave me from 1 Chronicles.

The final chapter of the book contains these lovely verses:

Yours, Lord, is the greatness and the power
and the glory and the majesty and the splendor,
for everything in heaven and earth is yours.
Yours, Lord, is the Kingdom;
you are exalted as head over all.
Wealth and honor come from you;
you are the ruler of all things.

In your hands are strength and power
to exalt and give strength to all.
Now, our God, we give you thanks,
and praise your glorious name.
1 Chronicles 29:11–13

As fallible humans with limited knowledge, power, and resources, we need frequent reminders of God's sovereignty. When we face challenges, we must remember that our Father is above every obstacle. The same God who governs the universe also guides the course of our lives. We might not know what our future holds, but our Father already has a perfect plan for our lives. We might not have enough money to pay our bills, but our Father owns all the resources in the world. We might fear a medical diagnosis, but our Father will heal the bodies he created, even if healing means bringing us into his presence.

Our Father is not a God of scarcity, but abundance. Through his generosity, we are empowered to walk through life with confidence because creation bows to his authority. He is infinitely powerful, and he endows us with the strength to overcome every obstacle. He owns all the resources in the universe, and he loves to share them with his children. Let's walk in the confident authority with which we are blessed today and every day!

Father, I confess that you are great and powerful. As the creator, ruler, and owner of the heavens and the earth, you deserve all the glory and majesty. I exalt you as head over everything, from the vastness of the universe to the finite confines of my life. As the only source of true riches, honor, and strength, I thank you for sharing your resources with me. I am humbled by your love, and I praise your glorious name and the name of your Son, Jesus. Amen.

Personal Reflection

Prayerfully reflect upon any needs in your life: financial, relational, physical, emotional, mental, or otherwise. Write 2-4 of your top needs below, then pray over each. Ask God for provision, but also confess your faith that he will provide exactly what you need at exactly the right moment. Praise him in advance for sharing his strength and provision with you.

_____

_____

_____

_____

_____

_____

_____

_____

_____

_____

_____

_____

_____

Day 36

Lemon Drops

Yesterday we discussed the generosity of God. As his children, we are called to reflect his character and transform increasingly into his image. When he calls us to give generously and serve selflessly, it isn't because he is running low on supplies or too tired to help out. God wants us to become more like him and, in so doing, draw closer to him. When we walk closely with him, we are blessed as we simultaneously become a blessing to others. Allow me to illustrate by means of my lemon drops.

Each spring, my primrose lemon drops begin to emerge. By early summer, a roughly 5x10 foot portion of my garden is covered in the bright yellow blooms. The flowers are special to me because they were a gift from my friend Doug, who shared them from his own garden. Doug, himself, had obtained the flowers from an aunt with whom he was especially close, so they were likewise meaningful to him. Because the lemon drops grow and proliferate wherever they are planted, sharing them doesn't exhaust the supply. Instead, the more the flowers are shared, the more they grow. And in fact, I've shared them with several friends of my own.

My point is that our resources can multiply similarly. Although our time, money, and energy seem finite, if we place them in God's hands, we'll never run out. Often, when we see other people prosper, we are tempted to feel jealous or angry. Instead of celebrating their success, we become resentful. We might even go so far as to slander them or place stumbling blocks in their path. However, we needn't be worried that the success of another makes our own prosperity less likely. Our Father has plenty of blessings for all of his children. In fact, when we bless others, we open ourselves up to greater blessings from the Lord. According to Proverbs 22:9a, "Blessed are those who are generous." God says, similarly, in Genesis 12:3a, "I will bless those who bless you." Although he was speaking specifically to Abraham, the principle pertains to all of us. God loves to bless people who bless others.

So let's live according to the principle of the lemon drops. Let's share freely and watch our generosity multiply into a beautiful garden of blessings.

Father, thank you for freely sharing your love and grace even though I don't deserve them. Teach me to reflect your character such that I generously share my own resources. I repent of selfishness, covetousness, and jealousy. Empower me to entrust all my resources to you and use them as you lead me. I ask you to open my eyes to opportunities to bless others today. In Jesus' name, Amen.

Personal Reflection

Be intentional to show generosity and bless others today.

_____

_____

_____

_____

_____

Day 37
I Will Always Love You

The last couple of days, we've discussed God's generosity and our call to emulate his character. As he works through us, his blessings are multiplied exponentially. In sum, God loves to bless his children because he loves us deeply.

The Hebrew word that describes God's unconditional love for his people is *hesed*. Difficult to translate into English, the term expresses "love, mercy, grace, kindness, goodness, benevolence, loyalty, [and] covenant faithfulness." *Hesed* isn't simply a warm fuzzy emotion. It represents the force that motivates a person to take selfless action for the benefit of another without expecting anything in return.

Hesed is found throughout the Old Testament, and the book of Ruth offers an excellent illustration of the concept. The narrative opens tragically as Naomi is faced with the death of her husband and two sons. Since women of her time and culture had few options for providing for themselves in the absence of a man, the situation was dire. Nonetheless, Naomi selflessly released her two daughters-in-law to return to their families and remarry. As she extended *hesed* to the two young women, she prayed that God would extend his own *hesed* and grant them security. Although one daughter-in-law returned home, Ruth exhibited *hesed* by staying with Naomi and even leaving her own country to live with her mother-in-law in Judah.

As the narrative progresses, Ruth is met with the *hesed* of Boaz as he allows her to glean from his fields so that she and Naomi have food to eat. Discovering that he is a relative of her deceased husband, Naomi plays matchmaker and encourages Ruth to pursue Boaz, who responds with joy. He says,

> *"The Lord bless you, my daughter!" Boaz exclaimed.*
> *"You are showing even more [hesed] now than you did*
> *before, for you have not gone after a younger man,*
> *whether rich or poor. Now don't worry about a thing,*
> *my daughter. I will do what is necessary, for everyone*
> *in town knows you are a virtuous woman." . . . So*
> *Boaz took Ruth into his home, and she became his*
> *wife. When he slept with her, the Lord enabled her to*
> *become pregnant, and she gave birth to a son. Then*
> *the women of the town said to Naomi, "Praise the*
> *Lord, who has now provided a redeemer for your family! May this child be famous in Israel. May he restore*
> *your youth and care for you in your old age. For he is*
> *the son of your daughter-in-law who loves you and*
> *has been better to you than seven sons!"*
>
> ### Ruth 3:10–11; 4:13–15

Naomi's *hesed* toward Ruth triggered a chain reaction of kindness that blessed both Ruth and Boaz and eventually looped back around to bless Naomi, herself. In fact, through *hesed* generations were blessed as Ruth's son became the grandfather of King David.

When we embody the deep and enduring love of God, his blessings flow beyond measure. Although we don't extend kindness for the purpose of getting anything in exchange, our selfless service can create a chain reaction of joy and generosity that blesses us in return. Let's take every opportunity to extend *hesed* today!

Father, thank you for your selfless gift of salvation. I pray you would help me better reflect your hesed love to the world. Open my eyes to opportunities to spread kindness and extend generosity. Teach me to give and serve with no expectation of reward. I pray that as I extend hesed, others would be inspired to give their own selfless service and love. In Jesus' name, Amen.

Personal Reflection

Once again, seek to show generosity and bless others today. Be especially intentional about serving and expecting nothing in return.

_____

_____

_____

_____

_____

_____

_____

_____

_____

_____

_____

_____

_____

Day 38
Mint Condition

Mint grows in a multitude of varieties and offers an abundance of benefits. Unfortunately, the plant is aggressively invasive. I strongly caution against planting mint in your garden. Even potted mint must be watched closely, as the rapidly growing strands will seek out the soil and root themselves. Without close supervision, mint will grow completely out of control and dominate every inch of ground.

The nature of mint reminds me of the principle of self-control. Mint is beneficial when kept in check and grown in moderation, like many aspects of life. For example, food is necessary and beneficial for our physical health. Yet, a lack of self-control in our eating habits can become sin and cause health problems. Sexual appetites, likewise, are healthy when fulfilled in the context of marriage. Yet, allowing sexual desires to go unchecked leads to debasement, addiction, and disease. Even exercise can be harmful in excess.

Paul teaches about the importance of self-control in numerous passages. In Titus, he specifically reminds us that our salvation empowers us to live a self-controlled and holy life. He exhorts,

> *For the grace of God has been revealed as salvation to all people, training us to deny ungodliness and worldly desires, so that we would live self-controlled and righteously and godly in the present age, looking forward to the blessed hope and appearing of the glory*

of our great God and Savior, Jesus Christ, who gave himself for us, in order to redeem us from all lawlessness and to purify for himself a people for his own possessions, zealous to do good deeds.

Titus 2:11–14, my translation

Instead of allowing our base desires to consume us, we can cultivate the divine gift of self-control. Although keeping our spiritual garden free of invasive habits takes mental energy, in the long run we save ourselves the toil of uprooting unwanted overgrowth.

Just as keeping my mint trimmed and contained allows me to cultivate numerous other beneficial and beautiful plants, cultivating a tidy spiritual garden creates room for personal growth. As Paul explains, maintaining self-control by keeping our eyes on our Savior empowers us to direct our energy toward growing in faith and doing good deeds. Let's sow seeds of self-control before unwanted overgrowth has a chance to invade the garden of our souls.

Jesus, thank you for empowering me to overcome temptation. Grow my capacity for self-control as I seek to cultivate a healthy spiritual garden. Help me turn from overt sin as well as transgressions that are often ignored, such as overindulgence in food, abusing my body through excess exercise, or completely neglecting to exercise. Reveal any areas of my life in which I am tending toward excess or a lack of self-discipline. Empower me to become healthier and more obedient out of love rather than fear or guilt. In Jesus' name, Amen.

Personal Reflection

Prayerfully consider whether you are struggling with self-discipline or self-control in any areas of your life. Ask God to reveal one pattern of behavior that is threatening to clutter your spiritual garden. Determine one step you can take toward tidying your garden or uprooting invasive overgrowth. Write your plan below and practice every day this week.

_____

_____

_____

_____

_____

_____

_____

_____

_____

_____

_____

_____

_____

_____

_____

_____

Day 39

Sin City — Part 1

In the next several devotionals, we'll delve into more serious territory than usual. I hope you'll stick with me until we return to more lighthearted fare in a few days.

Yesterday we discussed the topic of self-control, and today we'll shift to the related issues of steadfast obedience, holiness, and faithfulness. To illustrate, I'd like to tell you about the church at Thessalonica, a thriving, cosmopolitan city in ancient Rome.

Due to its coastal location, the city housed a diverse population with an assortment of cults. Inhabitants of Thessalonica, and most other Roman cities, welcomed nearly any religion as long as its followers were willing to worship the Roman emperor. The monotheism taught by preachers of the Gospel, like Paul, was perplexing to Roman citizens, who had trouble understanding why Christians couldn't worship Christ *and* the emperor *and* the myriad of other deities.

Thus, the mindset shift from rampant idolatry to the worship of Christ alone was monumental. In contrast to the way you and I perceive conversion, the radical reorientation demanded by Paul often resulted in social ostracism, emotional distress, and persecution. Conversion into the community of faith was a radical step that involved a whole new—greatly reduced—social status and alternative way of life. Although persecution wasn't official until later decades, the social and occupational ostracism accompanied by conversion often rendered believers unable to find work and provide for their families. Modern "cancel culture," for example, offers a familiar parallel.

Despite the difficulties, however, the new believers in the Thessalonian church received the Gospel with joy and lived out their faith with conviction. In his first epistle to the young church, Paul celebrates their steadfastness: "So you received the message with joy from the Holy Spirit in spite of the severe suffering it brought you. In this way, you imitated both us and the Lord. As a result, you have become an example to all the believers in Greece—throughout both Macedonia and Achaia," (1 Thessalonians 1:6–7). The steadfastness of the church is even more impressive considering the dramatic life change their new faith would have required.

Because of their courage, holiness, and perseverance, members of the Thessalonian church had an impact on the world around them. Their example encouraged fellow believers and demonstrated the love of God to non-believers. We'll discuss specifics tomorrow, but let's pause for today and consider our own lifestyle.

Although our culture was once based on Judeo-Christian principles, we are moving increasingly far from that foundation. We must consider whether we, as Christ-followers, are willing to live differently than our peers? Do we have the courage to reject compromise? Will we stand on *the* truth or kneel on the altar of compromise?

Jesus, thank you for your example of steadfast faith. Teach me likewise to be an example of faith among my family, my peers, and my community. Give me the courage to stand up for biblical principles, even those which are unpopular. Help me live in holiness so that I am set apart from the immoral practices of my culture. Teach me to dialogue with and show love to people with whom I disagree without compromising my faith. In Jesus' name, Amen.

Personal Reflection

Our society increasingly condones practices and beliefs that are contrary to biblical values. Prayerfully consider how you respond to cultural norms that conflict with the Christian faith. Do you, like the Thessalonians, refuse to compromise in the face of societal pressure? Or do you go with the flow and keep the peace to avoid conflict and scorn? Do you speak the truth (with love) in difficult situations? Or do you condone blatantly unbiblical ideologies in order to fit in with your peers? Remember that there is no condemnation in Christ, yet our Lord offers stern reprimands to believers who compromise their faith.

_____

_____

_____

_____

_____

_____

_____

_____

_____

_____

_____

_____

Day 40
Sin City — Part 2

Yesterday we began discussing the first-century church at Thessalonica, which Paul applauds for its faith and holiness. Today, we'll talk specifically about sexual purity, and the positive example that members of the Thessalonian church provided for us.

Although I was hesitant to write a devotional about sexual sin, I felt compelled by the state of our culture and the condition of the Western church. Statistics suggest that a third of men and a quarter of women *in the church* have committed adultery. In a 2020 survey by the Pew Research center, more than 50% of evangelical believers indicated that casual sex, "between consenting adults who are not in a committed romantic relationship" is sometimes or always acceptable. Equally distressing, pornography addictions are rampant—even among church members.

For the early church, much like the Western church today, remaining faithful in the midst of a non-Christian, sex-saturated culture was difficult. To make matters worse, ceremonies honoring the emperor and other pagan gods—a regular part of Greco-Roman life—typically included sexual activities. For members of the Christian community, such activities were untenable on multiple levels.

To explain in greater depth, allow me to direct your attention to the forebearers of Christianity, the Jewish people. The Jewish faith centered around the Jerusalem temple, a masterpiece of ancient architecture. The splendor of the holy precinct reflected the glory of God and was considered an earthly home for God's presence. The temple was the focal point of the Jewish faith as well as a tangible and visible reminder that God dwelt among his people.

The burgeoning Christian community had no such focal point. Instead, Jesus taught that the body of each individual believer was a temple. Jesus had, indeed, moved the location of sacred space from the temple to the body. The ability to worship God and experience his presence anywhere set the early Christians apart from their pagan and Jewish neighbors. Yet, the lack of a central location for the new faith introduced an instability that traditional religions did not face. In the absence of a tangible focal point for their faith, personal and communal holiness was the binding agent of the early church.

Thus, returning to our original topic of purity, sexual sin had the potential to inflict severe damage upon the early Christian community. Paul's words to the Thessalonian church reflect the gravity of the issue. He teaches,

> *God's will is for you to be holy, so stay away from all sexual sin. Then each of you will control his own body and live in holiness and honor—not in lustful passion like the pagans who do not know God and his ways. Never harm or cheat a fellow believer in this matter by violating his wife, for the Lord avenges all such sins, as we have solemnly warned you before. God has called us to live holy lives, not impure lives. Therefore, anyone who refuses to live by these rules is not disobeying human teaching but is rejecting God, who gives his Holy Spirit to you. But we don't need to write to you about the importance of loving each other, for God himself has taught you to love one another.*
>
> **1 Thessalonians 4:3–9**

Paul warns that defiling the body with sexual sin is to behave as one who doesn't know God, and that repeated sexual sin is akin to rejecting God himself! Sexual immorality is especially egregious for believers because the offense is committed in the very temple of God—our bodies.

Along such lines, sexual sin dishonors God, debases those who participate, creates instability within the faith community, and harms the witness of the church. Alternately, when community members live in holiness and purity, they reflect the character of the Father, fostering cohesion and love within the family of faith. We'll continue the topic tomorrow, but for now, please understand that my intention is not to condemn. My purpose is to shine light on *why* God calls us to a life of purity and equip you with the knowledge to succeed.

Father, thank you for teaching me how to keep my heart healthy and holy. Give me the self-discipline to avoid every type of sexual sin. Help me guard my body and my mind. I pray that you would take away any desire to view or engage in sexual immorality and instead make it repulsive to me. Give me such love and respect for my fellow humans that I can't bear to see them degraded. Help me be an example of love and holiness in my culture. In Jesus' name, Amen.

Personal Reflection

Prayerfully reflect on your attitude toward sexual sin. If you have any secret sins, unconfessed affairs, or areas of sexual addiction, pray for the courage to repent to God and talk to a pastor or trusted spiritual leader. If sexual sin isn't an overt struggle for you, consider whether you might be putting yourself in danger of temptation via television, movies, or other forms of entertainment. Might you need to make any changes regarding your media consumption? If you truly feel no conviction, pray for the attitude of our culture toward sex and pray for God to work in the hearts of his people to restore a culture of purity.

_____

_____

_____

_____

_____

_____

_____

_____

_____

_____

_____

_____

_____

_____

_____

Day 41
Sin City — Part 3

The last few days, we've talked about self-discipline and holiness with a special focus on sexual purity. The first-century Thessalonian church provides a shining example, and Paul's letter to them helps us understand why adhering to God's standards for sexuality is vital for our spiritual health. Yesterday we read the New Living Translation of 1 Thessalonians 4:3–9. Today, I'd like to look at a more literal translation of the passage.

> *For this is the will of God: your sanctification—that you abstain from sexual sin, that each of you learn to control your own vessel with holiness and honor, not in lustful passion like the gentiles who don't know God, not transgressing and exploiting your brothers and sisters in the matter, because the Lord is an avenger concerning all these things, just as we already told you and solemnly warned you. For God has not called us for the purpose of impurity, but for holiness. Therefore, the one who refuses does not reject man, but the God who places his Holy Spirit in you. But concerning love for brothers and sisters, you don't need anyone to write to you because you yourselves are taught by God to love one another.*

1 Thessalonians 4:3–9, my translation

Why is sexual sin so harmful to individual believers and to the body of Christ? The first, and most obvious, manner in which one might harm a brother or sister is by transgressing the boundaries of God and the personhood of a fellow believer. Sexual sin disregards not only the holiness of God but also the dignity of others. The offense is grievous because it distorts the holy image of God in each individual.

Infidelity within a marriage is even more egregious. Sexual unfaithfulness breaks the marriage covenant, destroys the holiness of the union, and detrimentally impacts the spiritual, relational, and emotional health of every person in the family.

In short, sexual sin breaks the foremost command given by God: to love God and one another. The command to love God and neighbor is the foundation upon which the entire Gospel rests. In verse 9 above, Paul reminds his audience that love is the key to sanctification and communal wholeness. Lust, on the other hand, is an alluring substitute that erodes the foundation of the Gospel and degrades people made in God's image. Sexual sin, in any culture or time period, is divisive, destructive, and degrading. Fornication is a false substitute and ugly parody of God's greatest command of love.

The second manner in which sexual sin creates damage is less obvious. Because Paul seeks to build a faith community that is whole and holy, community members have a responsibility to the entire Body of Christ. Although Paul did not have access to modern neurological and anthropological research, scientific studies increasingly confirm the scriptural and anthropological understanding of group boundaries, which are essential to the health of any group, organization, or collective.

In case this concept is unfamiliar, allow me to explain. Personal experience and group boundaries create a "library of values" that guide behaviors. The library of acceptable behaviors is created as individuals observe other group members. Basically, group members observe other group members to determine which behaviors are acceptable. This process is typically subconscious, but nonetheless has a strong impact on the health of a community. Thus, when an individual behaves in a manner that is inconsistent with group identity, they weaken communal stability and increase the potential for other members to behave inconsistently. If not corrected, the dysfunction can actually create a new group identity that is characterized by dysfunction and hypocrisy. For any church trying to survive in the midst of a non-believing culture, adding internal dysfunction to the external pressure can be a fatal blow. Only through maintaining clear purity standards can the church survive and grow in the midst of a sex-saturated culture.

Finally, the third avenue along which sexual sin creates harm is the witness of the Church. In modern Western culture, sex has become its own idol, functioning as the cornerstone of various ideologies and masquerading under the banner of love. Instead, the Church must demarcate clear boundaries in order to show the world the Gospel and the true nature of love.

Paul's paradigm for holiness and growth is beautifully self-perpetuating. As members of the community grow in sanctification out of love for God and fellow humans, group health is established, and adherence to God's commands becomes the automatic response of each member. As the individuals and the community grow in holiness and health, those outside the group respond favorably. In the first century, as today, the love and wholeness of the church commends the Gospel to those who need it most.

Father, thank you for teaching me the true nature of love. Teach me to be holy without becoming self-righteous and to be pure without becoming prideful. I pray that you would continue to grow my capacity for self-discipline and self-control. Enable me to see my fellow humans through your eyes so that I'm not tempted to debase them or myself by watching or engaging in sexual licentiousness. Help me to live in purity so that I can likewise show your love to the world. In Jesus' name, Amen.

Personal Reflection

As you did yesterday, continue to reflect on your attitude toward sexual sin. If you have any secret sins, unconfessed affairs, or areas of sexual addiction, reach out to a pastor or trusted spiritual leader and schedule a time to talk. Otherwise, continue to pray about whether you need to make any changes in the entertainment or media you consume. Finally, continue to pray for the attitude of our culture toward sex and for the purity of the church.

_____

_____

_____

_____

_____

_____

_____

_____

_____

_____

_____

_____

Day 42
Heigh-Ho, Heigh-Ho — Part 1

We spent the last several days discussing the exemplary purity of the Thessalonian church. Yet, despite the holiness and perseverance of the church members, they weren't perfect. In the final chapter of his Thessalonian correspondence, Paul pointed out a flaw in the culture of the church. He writes,

> *And now, dear brothers and sisters, we give you this command in the name of our Lord Jesus Christ: Stay away from all believers who live idle lives and don't follow the tradition they received from us. For you know that you ought to imitate us. We were not idle when we were with you. We never accepted food from anyone without paying for it. We worked hard day and night so we would not be a burden to any of you. We certainly had the right to ask you to feed us, but we wanted to give you an example to follow. Even while we were with you, we gave you this command: "Those unwilling to work will not get to eat." Yet we hear that some of you are living idle lives, refusing to work and meddling in other people's business. We command such people and urge them in the name of the Lord Jesus Christ to settle down and work to earn*

their own living. As for the rest of you, dear brothers
and sisters, never get tired of doing good.
2 Thessalonians 3:6–13

Many of the Thessalonian believers were out of work and mooching off fellow community members. Whether they had quit their jobs or been fired for their faith is unknown. Yet, instead of seeking out new opportunities to provide for themselves, they were simply sitting around and allowing other people to support them.

Based on Paul's instructions in 2 Thessalonians, scholars conjecture that the Thessalonian believers expected Jesus to return soon. Thus, rather than seeking to earn a living, some members of the congregation were simply waiting around, taking advantage of fellow believers, and causing trouble. Paul bluntly rebukes such behavior. He teaches that since we don't know when the Lord will return (1 Thessalonians 5:2), we should avoid idleness, work hard, and persevere in doing good. When we stay busy with God's will, we won't have time to gossip, meddle, or get into trouble.

Just as many of the Thessalonian believers avoided work, our culture seems to have an increasing aversion to meaningful labor. As the body of Christ, we are called to model a healthy work ethic and commitment to service. Salvation might be a free gift, but we still have to earn a living! Let's honor our Lord by working productively and building his Kingdom.

Father, thank you for giving me the ability and opportunity to earn a living. Forgive me for taking employment and meaningful labor for granted. Help me to seek out and maintain purposeful work habits even when I don't like the opportunities around me or my current workplace. Give me the grit and fortitude to work even when I don't feel like it. Equip me to provide for myself so that I can help others and be a blessing to your Kingdom. In Jesus' name, Amen.

Personal Reflection

Prayerfully reflect on your attitude toward employment, work, and service. Do you provide for yourself and/or contribute to your household? Do you seek to honor God by working hard and doing your best or do you try to get by with a bare minimum of effort? Ask God to reveal one area you haven't been giving your best in supporting yourself, your family, or his Kingdom. Write your thoughts below so you can reference them tomorrow.

_____

_____

_____

_____

_____

_____

_____

_____

_____

_____

_____

_____

Day 42

_____

_____

_____

_____

_____

_____

_____

_____

_____

_____

_____

_____

_____

_____

_____

_____

_____

_____

Day 43
Heigh-Ho, Heigh-Ho — Part 2

Yesterday we discussed the importance of work in our life and faith. Today, I'd like to offer more theological scaffolding. The mention of "work" elicits a generally negative reaction, but in Scripture, work does not necessarily denote toil. Instead of portraying work negatively, biblical authors describe work as a generally productive and healthy activity. In fact, the term is used to describe God's creative activity in Genesis.

When undertaken by humans, work is a means by which we cultivate mutually beneficial connections with one another and the rest of creation. Instead of draining us, healthy work contributes meaningfully to the world and fosters a sense of satisfaction, thankfulness, and interconnectedness.

In my opinion, a prime factor that contributes to our dislike of work is that we view labor as a means of increasing personal comfort. What if, instead, we viewed work as a God-given appointment? Paul instructs, "Work willingly at whatever you do, as though you were working for the Lord rather than for people. Remember that the Lord will give you an inheritance as your reward, and that the Master you are serving is Christ," (Colossians 3:23–24). We should work as if we are working for the Lord because we are, in fact, working for the Lord. No matter who we work for or where we are employed, our true master is God himself. And our labor isn't simply for the purpose of earning a paycheck or furthering our careers. As we work, we represent our Savior and share his love with the world. Through our labor, we strive to make our communities and our world a better place.

Let me offer myself as an example. Right now, I *want* to take a nap, but I *should* press on and continue writing. If I were working for my own benefit, my own profit, or my own comfort, I would probably quit writing, snuggle up with my dogs, and go to sleep. If making myself happier is my goal, I'll always choose the option that is most appealing to *me*. If, however, my goal is to honor God and minister to his people, I'll be much more likely to persevere through the task at hand.

Now, some especially disciplined, yet faithless, individuals are able to push through discomfort and work hard for the sake of long-term personal gains. However, without a deeper purpose, every accomplishment is as empty and meaningless as the last. The fast-food worker who flips burgers while sharing the Gospel will find more fulfillment than the wealthiest mogul or movie star who doesn't know God. So, let's live purposefully, work hard, and make the most of every opportunity to honor our Father with our very best efforts.

Lord, thank you for giving us your best while you walked on this earth, and thank you for the examples of hard-working men and women in Scripture. Give me a greater determination to work hard and serve faithfully. Empower me to give my best even when I'm weary. Teach me to find a healthy balance between work and rest. Help me learn when to press on and when to slow down. I desire to honor you in the way I conduct myself each day. In your name, Amen.

Personal Reflection

Yesterday you reflected upon your attitude toward work and prayed for God to reveal one area in which you haven't been giving your best. Review your notes from yesterday and pray for God to help you determine a specific strategy for working more purposefully. Write down your plan then begin to implement it today!

Day 44
Bandit

Bandit is a ceramic racoon that Wesley purchased for me on Mother's Day. When I opened the gift and saw Bandit's cute little face, I couldn't wait to find the perfect spot in my garden for him. After much thought, I decided to nestle him among the potted ivy on my front porch. I imagined that he would be a cute and fun surprise for anyone who saw him peeking from among the plants.

However, Bandit surprised me far more often than any guests who visited our home. Because I spend most of my time in the back yard or on the back patio, I tend to forget about Bandit. Thus, over the course of several months following Bandit's arrival, he frightened me every time I approached the front porch. On countless occasions, I experienced momentary panic over the husky woodland animal crouched by my front door.

I refused to relocate Bandit because each time I encountered the raccoon, I was certain I would never again be startled by him. Surely, I thought, I'm well accustomed to his presence by now. Yet, each time I passed by, he surprised me afresh.

Sadly, we often handle our struggles in the same way I handled Bandit. We continue to make the same mistakes and struggle with the same problems over and over again, hoping that we'll eventually overcome them. At the same time, we don't do anything to facilitate change. The author of Proverbs teaches, "As a dog returns to its vomit, so a fool repeats his foolishness," (Proverbs 26:11). If we want a different result, we have to do something differently. According to a modern aphorism, "If you do what you always did, you'll get what you always got."

Just as I realized that I would have to find a new location for Bandit to reside, I realized that I would have to change something if I wanted to overcome my bad habits. Hoping that next time will be different or expecting that healthier habits will develop by sheer force of will simply isn't realistic. If we hope to improve any aspect of our physical, mental, or spiritual health, we must take steps that are prayerful, intentional, and meaningful. We'll discuss how to identify and implement effective strategies for change over the next couple of days. For today, simply pray, meditate, and identify your own "bandits."

Lord, thank you for loving me no matter how many times I repeat the same mistakes. Help me institute meaningful change as I seek to walk along paths of wisdom instead of foolishness. Show me areas of my life in which I tend to stumble over and over again. I pray that my sins would become as repugnant as vomit so that I no longer desire to return to those behaviors. Grow my love for you so that my desire for your presence overcomes any desires to walk down self-destructive or harmful paths. Give me a desire to make healthy changes so that I can live in freedom and follow you with joy. In Jesus' name, Amen.

Personal Reflection

Prayerfully meditate on recurring patterns of thought or behaviors that you can't seem to change. Simply ask God to help you identify a few "bandits" and write them below.

Day 44

Day 45
Racoon Robbers — Part 1

Yesterday we talked about my fake racoon, Bandit. I much prefer owning a ceramic racoon to a real one. Raccoons are among the most renowned thieves of the animal kingdom. The masked bandits will not only steal food, but they love to abscond with anything shiny. Even worse, the curious creatures will rummage through your garbage, garden, and potted plants to search for anything they might want to take. Whether or not they discover any good loot, they often leave a trail of destruction in their wake. As we discussed in one of our winter devos, racoons will even damage your home, chewing through electrical wiring, ripping out insulation, and tearing through shingles.

Much like racoons, the Enemy wants to steal from us and wreak destruction in our lives. Describing the intent of Satan, Jesus says, "The thief comes only to steal and kill and destroy," (John 10:10a). We have an Enemy who wants to steal our freedom, kill our joy, and destroy our futures. Although we can't see him, we can see the results of his schemes. Much like racoons who root through your trash and steal your goods during the night, our Enemy works under the cover of darkness. Resultantly, we either blame ourselves, devolving into a mindset of guilt and shame, or blame others, creating relational strife. In reality, we need to be fighting the Enemy instead of berating ourselves or battling our brothers and sisters.

Identifying our true Enemy is crucial if we want to make meaningful changes and maintain lasting growth. As Jesus said, "The thief comes only to steal and kill and destroy; *I have come that they may have life, and have it to the full,"* (John 10:10, emphasis mine). Jesus defeated Satan on your behalf, but he also died on the cross for *all* people. Other people are never your enemies! Let's turn on the floodlights and get rid of the real source of the problems in our lives.

Lord, thank you for making a full, abundant life available to me. Enable me to see through the schemes and lies of the Enemy. Forgive me for condemning myself and battling other people instead of my true adversary. Give me the wisdom and the strength to identify the root causes of my struggles and sins. Empower me to walk in joy and health as I take back what the Enemy has stolen. In Jesus' name, Amen.

Personal Reflection

Yesterday, you worked on identifying pesky bandits in your life who keep you from transformation and sanctification. Today, prayerfully meditate on the true sources of your struggle. Have you allowed the Enemy to steal the truth from your mind and replace it with his lies? Are you allowing him to strip the fruit of the spirit from your branches and replace them with a harvest of bitterness, worry, and strife? For each bandit you wrote down yesterday, identify how the Enemy is at work in the shadows. What lies have you believed and what has the Enemy stolen or destroyed as a result? Write down your thoughts so you can refer back to them tomorrow.

_____

_____

_____

_____

Day 46
Racoon Robbers — Part 2

The last couple of days, we've discussed racoons, little bandits who steal and destroy. Like racoons, the Enemy of our souls loves to steal, kill and destroy. His sneaky strategies often lead us into habits and behaviors that are difficult to change. We get stuck in harmful cycles that we can't seem to break, no matter how hard we try.

Unfortunately, trying harder is the least effective way to foster genuine and lasting change. We can, however, implement a few strategic changes and take a few intentional steps to prevent the Enemy from robbing our peace and stealing our purpose.

First, as we've already discussed, identify the bandits in your life—the patterns of thought and behavior that are stealing your spiritual health, destroying your relationships, and killing your joy. Part of that process is identifying your true Enemy, Satan, and the lies with which he has deceived you. Jesus teaches that when you know the truth, "the truth will set you free," (John 8:32). So, ask God to help you discern the truth about yourself, your fellow humans, your God, and your destructive cycles of sin.

Second, once you understand the truth, you can evaluate your "why." Why are you stuck in certain patterns, and why do you want to change? How will your life be better? How will your relationship with God be more fruitful? As you increasingly understand the truths that underlie your thoughts and actions as well as the benefits of change, your thoughts and behaviors begin to align with your will. In more scientific terms, the prefrontal cortex of the brain, which makes instantaneous decisions faster than conscious thought, begins to change its default from the behaviors that we *don't* want to the behaviors that we *do* want.

Third, ask for help and accountability. Honestly evaluating our own spiritual and mental state is extremely difficult. Because our struggles have a very real impact on our brain chemistry and cognitive abilities, we need help finding the truth! Seeking an objective perspective from a trusted friend or mentor can bring clarity in the midst of confusion. Further, just as understanding our "why" helps reset default decisions, healthy relationships likewise help to transform ingrained patterns of subconscious thought in the brain.

Fourth, professional counseling is a potent resource that is often ignored. For example, if my yard becomes infested with racoons, I'm going to call a specialist to help me get rid of them. Why would I struggle to fix the problem alone when those who have expertise and experience are available to help me?

I could list a hundred other strategies for making healthy change, most especially Bible Study, prayer, fasting, and other spiritual disciplines, but in short, your Father loves you and has placed a wealth of resources at your disposal. He is giving you the strength to take the first step and is ready to celebrate your growth. Seek his guidance and partner with him to exterminate the bandits and thieves from your life!

Father, thank you for offering grace that covers my sins, mistakes, and even the harmful behaviors that I repeat over and over again. Forgive me for going my own way and believing the lies of the Enemy. Empower me to see through his deception and understand the truth. Give me the strength and courage to take steps toward healing and health. Help me identify someone in my life who might be willing to offer wisdom and accountability. Give me a greater desire to live for you and honor you with my choices. In Jesus' name, Amen.

Personal Reflection

The last couple of days, you've listed your struggles, begun to identify the lies of the Enemy, and meditated on what he has stolen from you. Refer back to your notes from the past two days and then write out *why* you want to gain freedom in each area and what you'll take back from the Enemy. As you finish, prayerfully determine one or more changes you can make today to begin moving toward lasting health.

_____

_____

_____

_____

_____

_____

_____

_____

_____

_____

_____

_____

_____

Day 47
Yellow Finches

One sunny afternoon, I was watching several goldfinches flutter around my backyard. In case you aren't familiar, these petite birds are bright yellow and easy to spot. Yet, in the blink of an eye, they disappeared. I was mystified that the vibrant little birds seemed to have instantaneously vanished. As I scanned the yard, I soon spotted movement in a large patch of yellow flowers. I realized that the finches had landed in my flowers and were perfectly camouflaged.

The "disappearance" of the birds brought to my mind the multitude of verses in which our Father calls us to be set apart from the world. Like the finches, we often blend in with our surroundings instead of boldly shining the light of God's truth. As we've discussed over the last couple of weeks, God commands us to live differently than the culture by which we are surrounded. He calls us to walk in holiness, obedience, and sacrificial love rather than the debauchery endorsed by popular culture.

Just as we at times fail (often abysmally), the Judeans who returned to Judah after their exile fell into complacency and temptation. Their priestly leader, Ezra, received the following report:

> *Many of the people of Israel, and even some of the priests and Levites, have not kept themselves separate from the other peoples living in the land. They have taken up the detestable practices of the Canaanites,*

Hittites, Perizzites, Jebusites, Ammonites, Moabites, Egyptians, and Amorites. For the men of Israel have married women from these people and have taken them as wives for their sons.

Ezra 9:1b–2a

Instead of serving as a light to the nations, the returning exiles had become just like the nations. They had adopted abominable pagan practices and flagrantly disobeyed God's command against intermarriage. Ezra was so appalled that he tore his clothes, ripped hair from his head, collapsed to the ground, and wept (Ezra 9:3; 10:1). Ezra knew what we often fail to recognize—sin grieves the heart of God and often carries devastating consequences.

In the New Testament Paul expressed a similar principle. He warns:

Don't be fooled by those who try to excuse these sins, for the anger of God will fall on all who disobey him. Don't participate in the things these people do. For once you were full of darkness, but now you have light from the Lord. So live as people of light! For this light within you produces only what is good and right and true. Carefully determine what pleases the Lord. Take no part in the worthless deeds of evil and darkness; instead, expose them. It is shameful even to talk about the things that ungodly people do in secret. But their evil intentions will be exposed when the light shines on them, for the light makes everything visible.

Ephesians 5:6–14a

When we compromise our faith to blend in, we deprive the world of the peace and joy of God's Kingdom. We may even deprive people of the love of Christ.

Just as God called Israel to be a light to the nations, God created you to shine his light to the world! You are a masterpiece that reflects his glory. You are a bright light that allows others to see the truth. So don't disappear into the crowd like my finches camouflaged in the flowers.

Father, thank you for the extraordinary calling you have placed upon my life. Give me the boldness and courage to bear your light to the world. Teach me to be filled with the Holy Spirit so that I'm not tempted by the darkness of popular culture. Give me the wisdom to know when to speak and when to remain silent. Empower me to speak words of truth seasoned with love and grace. I pray that you would reveal any areas of my life in which I am failing to represent you well. Give me a desire to reject compromise and shine your light to the world. In Jesus' name, Amen.

Personal Reflection

Skim back over your notes from the last 10 days. Are there any sins or struggles that you can't seem to overcome? Are there any areas of life in which you consistently blend in with culture and fail to shine God's light? Are there any patterns of thought that you know don't reflect God's truth, but you still can't overcome. If so, you might be battling a deeply-seeded stronghold. Think back to *when* the struggle first began and *why* you felt compelled to behave or think that way. Write your thoughts below so you can reference them tomorrow.

Day 47

Day 48
Clear the Air

One morning, as I set out on my bicycle, I knew that the weather forecast called for clear blue skies, but I could see nothing but fog. Initially, the fog was so thick that I could barely see the road. My clothes became damp, and my skin was covered in droplets of water. As I continued to ride, however, the sun began to burn away the fog. My vision became clearer, and the landscape around me began to appear. Eventually, the fog lifted completely, and I could see clearly in every direction. As I gazed at the blue sky, green fields, and verdant trees, I thanked God for my beautiful surroundings.

As I pondered the process of navigating through the fog, I thought about the nature of sin. In some ways, our sin is much like a fog. When we first come to Christ, receive him as Lord, and accept his forgiveness, we embark upon a wonderful journey. Our sins are completely forgiven as the grace of God covers over our mistakes. But our forgiveness doesn't mean that we never again commit a sin or do things that grieve God's heart.

In other words, beginning our walk with Christ is a bit like setting off into a foggy landscape. We don't quite know what to expect, but we know that the sun is shining above. As we begin to learn about God and grow in faith, we are still surrounded by the fog of wrong patterns of thought and impure patterns of behavior. Over time, as we continue to walk with Jesus, he begins to lift the fog by gently and lovingly correcting harmful thoughts and behaviors. The more diligently we journey with him and allow him to work in our lives, the clearer our vision becomes and the better we see his glorious light through the clouds. This process of sanctification will last our entire lifetime, but the end result will be to see him in full, just as when the sun appears from behind the clouds and illuminates everything in beautiful light.

In the meantime, we are called to live in God's light and reflect that light to the world. According to 1 John,

> This is the message we heard from Jesus and now declare to you: God is light, and there is no darkness in him at all. So we are lying if we say we have fellowship with God but go on living in spiritual darkness; we are not practicing the truth. But if we are living in the light, as God is in the light, then we have fellowship with each other, and the blood of Jesus, his Son, cleanses us from all sin. If we claim we have no sin, we are only fooling ourselves and not living in the truth. But if we confess our sins to him, he is faithful and just to forgive us our sins and to cleanse us from all wickedness.

1 John 1:5–9

As we allow God to burn away our sin, just as the sun burns away the morning fog, his light shines increasingly through our lives. Let's submit to our Lord, continue walking with him, and watch as his love, plan, and purpose become ever more vibrant in our lives.

Lord, I am thankful that your blood covers every sin I have committed in the past and every sin that I will commit in the future. Help me honor your sacrifice by growing in holiness every day. Give me a greater desire to be transformed and sanctified so that I can see your light more clearly and better reflect your light to the world. I repent of getting stuck in the fog of sin, worry, and strife. Teach me to diligently walk with you even when I can't see the path before me. I ask you to reveal any specific areas of my life that are not honoring you. Help me overcome those areas through the power of your Spirit in me. Thank you for your patient guidance, mercy, and grace. In Jesus' name, Amen.

Personal Reflection

Yesterday, you began to identify persistent strongholds and struggles that are impeding your sanctification. Continue to consider *when* each struggle began and *why* you felt compelled to behave or think that way. Write down any additional insights the Spirit brings to your mind. Pray over each, then identify a friend, pastor, or Christian counselor with whom you can share your struggle. You may also want to engage in a fast in order to facilitate your process of freedom (Isaiah 58:6).

_____

_____

_____

_____

_____

_____

_____

Day 49
In the Light

At my parents' lake house, the dock is a steep walk down the hill across rocky terrain. During the day, when the sun is shining, the trek is no problem. At night after we gather around the fire pit, however, getting back to the house can be a challenge. In the absence of light to guide our way, the path is virtually invisible. We trip over branches and stumble over rocks as we navigate back to the house.

Without light, the distinct planes of existence are difficult to discern. Whether literally or metaphorically, light helps us see clearly. Line, shape, and texture become visible when light reveals that which surrounds us. Light illuminates the truth and exposes lies.

The psalmist praises God for shining his guiding light upon our lives. According to 119:105, "Your word is a lamp to guide my feet and a light for my path." The incarnate Word of God, our Savior, similarly taught, "I am the light of the world. If you follow me, you won't have to walk in darkness, because you will have the light that leads to life," (John 8:12b). What a gift and blessing that we don't have to stumble through life in the dark! Yet, we must be proactive to remain in his light and his Word so that our purpose and path become clear. Let's seek the illumination of Christ so that we are empowered to take advantage of each opportunity and avoid each hazard along the journey of life.

Jesus, thank you for bringing light to the world. Teach me to walk in your light every day. I repent of walking in the darkness and neglecting to spend intentional time with you. Grow my desire to study your Word so that your purpose and plan for my life become increasingly clear. Help me be more disciplined to evaluate my choices in the light of your truth. Teach me to discern the difference between truth and falsehood as I seek to live more fully in your light. In your name, Amen.

Personal Reflection

Use the concordance you identified in Day 26 to look up Scripture passages about light. Write down everything you learn about the light of God and how it illuminates the best path for your life.

_____

_____

_____

_____

_____

_____

_____

_____

_____

_____

_____

Day 50
You Are the Light

Yesterday we discussed walking in the light of the Lord. Our Father offers life-giving illumination for our path if we simply follow him. But following him isn't always so simple. Furthermore, we are called to reflect his light and shine brightly, even when we don't feel like it.

God recently gave me the opportunity to live out this principle. The morning was beautiful, but the bright sunshine was at odds with the storm in my heart. I'd been deeply offended by a friend, and I was irritated that the beautiful weather didn't match my inner gloom. I wanted to move past my anger, but the offense felt like a dark shadow over my heart.

The day prior, I had begun reading through the book of Matthew, so on that morning, my quiet time began in Matthew 5—not coincidentally, I'm sure. Although the whole chapter spoke loudly to my vexed heart, God spoke most clearly through the following verses:

> *You are the light of the world—like a city on a hilltop that cannot be hidden. No one lights a lamp and then puts it under a basket. Instead, a lamp is placed on a stand, where it gives light to everyone in the house. In the same way, let your good deeds shine out for all to see, so that everyone will praise your heavenly Father. . . . You have heard the law that says, "Love your*

neighbor" and hate your enemy. But I say, love your enemies! Pray for those who persecute you! In that way, you will be acting as true children of your Father in heaven. For he gives his sunlight to both the evil and the good.

Matthew 5:14–16, 43–45a

You and I have a divine calling to shine God's light to the world. We don't have to—we get to. We have the opportunity to help other people encounter the Creator and Savior of the universe by reflecting his grace and kindness. We might sometimes fall short, but we should always strive to reflect his light more brilliantly.

I would love to say that when I read Matthew 5, my heart immediately changed. It didn't. Instead, I felt comforted that my Father spoke so clearly to my heart. I felt solace that my Savior understood my pain because he experienced offense far worse than I can imagine. So, although I still *felt* hurt and offended, through faith, the storm clouds in my heart began to clear because I knew that my Lord was walking closely by my side.

As I concluded my devotional time that morning, the words of Psalm 30 came to mind and brought more light to my darkened spirit. I hope they brighten your heart as well.

I will exalt you, Lord, for you rescued me.
You refused to let my enemies triumph over me.
O Lord my God, I cried to you for help,
and you restored my health.
You brought me up from the grave, O Lord.
You kept me from falling into the pit of death.

. . .

Weeping may last through the night,
but joy comes with the morning.
Psalm 30:1–3, 5b

Heavenly Father, thank you for rescuing me when I cry out to you. Help me remain faithful through every trial and offense. Equip me to walk in your light even when my heart feels dark. Teach me to cling to you instead of doing and saying things that bring further harm. I ask you to comfort my soul and heal my wounds. Grow my faith through each trial and empower me to reflect your light more brightly to the world. In Jesus' name, Amen.

Personal Reflection

Prayerfully reflect on your response to offense. Do you tend to retaliate and slander the one who hurt you? Or do you draw close to God and obey his Word? Do you allow your emotions to dictate your reactions, or do you submit your desires to God and respond in faith? Write your thoughts below then determine one practical strategy you can employ next time you are offended. For example, you could increase your time in prayer and Bible study, refuse to slander the one who hurt you, pray for the one who hurt you, look up verses that address your offense, or ask a mentor to pray for and with you.

_____

_____

_____

_____

Day 51
How Will I Know?

The last couple of days we discussed the light of God, which illuminates our path through life. Yet, even if we trust God to guide and direct the course of our lives, we sometimes struggle to discern his will. So, how can we ascertain the will of God?

I'll answer that question in a moment, but first, let me tell you about Saint Francis of Assisi, the patron saint of ecology who founded the Franciscan order in the early 1200s. The son of a wealthy merchant, Francis enjoyed a pampered and self-indulgent youth. However, by his mid-twenties, Francis realized the futility of pleasure-seeking, took a vow of poverty, and began traversing the countryside ministering to the poor.

Francis' humble, devout lifestyle soon attracted followers. Although the rules of the order would later be expanded and codified, their guiding principle was "to live in obedience and chastity, and without property, and to follow the doctrine and footsteps of our Lord Jesus Christ." This "First Rule" was based on a collection of Scriptures, most notably Matthew 16:24, "Then Jesus said to his disciples, 'If any of you wants to be my follower, you must give up your own way, take up your cross, and follow me.'"

Saint Francis understood that before we make grand plans or pursue worldly success, we should master the fundamentals of faith. He exhorted people to be obedient in daily tasks, to serve selflessly, and to forsake materialism. In short, Saint Francis taught his followers to be more like Jesus.

I'll tell you more about Saint Francis tomorrow, but let's pause and return to our original question: how can we ascertain the will of God? Our Savior makes the universal will of God clear through his earthly life, and our Father makes his universal will clear through the writings of Scripture. If we want to determine God's specific will for our lives, we simply need to remain faithful to his universal will. The more we walk in the intimacy of faithful obedience, the more clearly we will hear his voice in other matters. So, although there is no quick fix or shortcut to discerning God's master plan for our life, he has clearly illuminated our next steps. Let's walk in faithfulness to his will and Word today.

Father, thank you for providing clear steps of obedience in your Word, and Jesus, thank you for living out an example of faithfulness. Teach me to walk in your footsteps as I seek to obey God. Give me a heart to serve others instead of living for myself. I repent of going my own way instead of following you. Empower me to be faithful in the small things so that I am ready to be faithful in the big things. I ask you to reveal any selfishness, pride, covetousness, or rebellion in my heart. In Jesus' name, Amen.

Personal Reflection

Seek to be faithful in the small things today. Strive to exhibit humility, serve others, and be more like Christ in every task and interaction.

_____

_____

Day 51

Day 52
Saint Francis

Yesterday I introduced you to Saint Francis and the Franciscan Order that he founded. Today, I'd like to tell you more about the manner in which Francis lived and ministered. In addition to a lifetime of service to poor and needy humans, Saint Francis exhibited a deep and abiding love for God's creation. Francis referred to animals as his "brothers" and "sisters," extending the designation even to inanimate objects such as the sun and moon.

Stories of Francis' interactions with the natural world abound. In one notable legend, Francis saved the town of Grubbio, Italy from a feral wolf. The saint reportedly spoke with the wolf and discovered that it was attacking the town because it was hungry. When Francis instructed the townspeople to feed the wolf, the canine agreed to cease its attacks. According to another legend, the saint was awoken by a raven each morning in time for prayer services. If Francis wasn't feeling well, however, the bird would delay waking him so that he could rest and recover. Legend also holds that Francis often preached to the birds, who would draw near and give him their rapt attention. Yet other stories recount Francis saving trapped animals, helping injured creatures, and even moving worms from the road so they wouldn't get trampled.

While the legends surrounding Francis strain the bounds of credulity, he clearly loved God's creation and considered it worthy of care. He believed that creation teaches humanity about the Father, but that it also has its own value. In other words, nature doesn't simply exist for humanity to use; creation holds its own inherent worth.

Francis didn't worship creation, but rather worshiped with and through the natural world. He even went so far as to sing along with the cicadas, frogs, and birds, believing their song to be one of praise. I imagine the man was a bit eccentric, but we can learn much from his faithful example.

In sum, God's original plan for a sinless, harmonious world is most fully realized when humans praise God with the chorus of creation. As the Psalmist proclaims,

Shout joyful praises to God, all the earth!
Sing about the glory of his name!
Tell the world how glorious he is.
Say to God, "How awesome are your deeds!
Your enemies cringe before your mighty power.
Everything on earth will worship you;
they will sing your praises,
shouting your name in glorious songs."
Psalm 66:1–4

Let's strive to learn about God through each element of the natural world while we worship him with all the earth and praise him by caring for it!

Father, thank you for revealing your glory through your creation. Teach me to honor you by caring for your creatures. Help me to better understand your character and your will as I meditate upon the natural world. Empower me to learn from creation as I worship alongside each element of it. Transform me increasingly into the image of Christ as I seek to minister to humans, creatures, and creation. In Jesus' name, Amen.

Personal Reflection

Meditate on how drawing closer to God through the natural world might help you grow in obedience and maturity. Then, as we began yesterday, continue striving to be faithful in the small things: exhibit humility, serve others, and be more like Christ in every task and interaction.

_____

_____

_____

_____

_____

_____

_____

_____

_____

_____

_____

_____

Day 53
Calm Waters

A few days ago, I mentioned my parents' lake house. One of the best parts of spending time at the lake is the quiet serenity of the surroundings. I love to sit or lay on the dock and gaze at the still, calm water. Unless the kids are swimming and splashing around, the surface of the lake is like a smooth mirror, reflecting the trees and skies above. As I sit, I seek to match the tenor of my soul to that of the lake—not so difficult in such an idyllic setting.

Maintaining mental and emotional equilibrium during every-day life is not as easy a task. Our minds constantly churn, creating ripples, waves, and sometimes tsunamis of emotion. Whether in the home, the workplace, or anywhere else, we encounter situations that disrupt our peace. We become frustrated by difficult people, we stress about our finances, and we fret over our to-do lists. We worry about the future, we lament over the past, and we agonize over the present. Instead of maintaining a mindset that resembles the smooth surface of the lake, our souls are more akin to the churning waters on the fourth of July when the lake is full of speedboats, water-skiers, and drunk rednecks.

Like the lake on July fourth, we can't always control our external circumstances, but we can train ourselves to calm the churnings of the mind. As we discussed in an earlier devotional, the key to remaining at peace is to trust God to calm the wind and waves. According to Isaiah 26:3, "You will keep in perfect peace, all who trust in you, all whose thoughts are fixed on you!"

Although being intentional to calm our thoughts and emotions is important, simply *trying* harder will never fully bring peace to our souls. Mental discipline alone will never yield the all-surpassing peace of God. No matter how much we try to stay calm, count to ten, or take deep breaths, we simply can't calm the waves ourselves. Only by fixing our eyes on the source of peace, growing in faith, and learning to trust the Father can we becalm our churning minds.

Father, thank you for watching over me and protecting me so that I don't have to worry about my past, present, or future. Forgive me for entertaining emotions and thoughts that are based upon the lies of the Enemy. Teach me to trust in your sovereignty instead of worrying about what might or might not happen. Train me to fix my eyes on you rather than my problems. Grow my faith as I simultaneously foster the mental fortitude not to ruminate over problems or stew in anger. Help me become more disciplined to take captive thoughts that steal my peace and replace them with the truth of your Word. In Jesus' name, Amen.

Personal Reflection

Be mindful of your mental and emotional state today. Take note of interactions or situations that disrupt your peace. Begin training yourself to shift your attention to God in difficult moments. Practice replacing worried thoughts with affirmations of faith. Seek to dampen angry emotions with compassionate prayers. Each time your mind and emotions begin to churn, fix your spiritual gaze upon your Father, the source of all peace.

_____

_____

Day 53

Day 54
Red Rocks

In November 2022, I was blessed to visit Denver for the first time, and of course Red Rock Canyon was on my agenda. (My mom and I took a whole extra suitcase for winter hiking gear.) Once we arrived at the park, we determined the trail that best fit our time constraints and set out. Although the season was winter, the day was beautifully sunny and warm.

The massive, brightly colored rock formations are truly awe-inspiring. Their ruddy color is derived from iron oxide, the same chemical compound that tints rust and blood. Yet over time, water has washed various concentrations of the iron oxide away, creating a vibrant rainbow of red, orange and brown.

The same water has molded the rocks into sculptures that captivate the imagination. The experience of gazing upon their contours is a bit like identifying shapes in the clouds. Some formations are so distinct that they've earned names like "Frog Rock," "Ship Rock," and "Seat of Pluto."

In addition to the extraordinary rock formations, the park boasts an impressive array of plant and animal life. More than 45 different species of mammal and 100 species of bird have been identified in the park. Just as impressive, more than 600 species of plants grow in the canyon, 15 of which are unique to Red Rock.

In such an environment, one might be tempted to worship the natural world, as have many pagans throughout history. Yet, rather than worshiping creation, we should be even more inspired to worship the one who created such ecological diversity and beauty. Richard Bauckham, esteemed biblical scholar, affirms that our awe at the natural world should inspire us to worship God *with* creation. He writes that "the goal of God's creative and redemptive work is achieved when every creature in heaven, on earth, under the earth and in the sea joins in a harmony of praise to God and the Lamb." Although the non-human creation doesn't worship through words or prayers, they offer praise simply by existing and reflecting God's handiwork.

In such a context, Jesus' words in Luke 19:40 come more clearly into focus. In the passage, Luke describes Jesus' triumphal entry into Jerusalem. As the crowds praised the Messiah and hailed him as King, some of the Pharisees rebuked Jesus and demanded that he silence his followers. Luke records, "So Jesus responded and said, 'I tell you, if these people become silent, the stones will shout with praise,'" (Luke 19:40). Although Jesus was speaking hyperbolically, he nonetheless offered theological truth: creation itself shouts praise without uttering a sound.

When we worship God, we join with the chorus of creation. Such an awareness should foster a more profound experience of worship not only during moments of intentional praise, but in every waking moment. Whether we are hiking through the mountains, strolling on the beach, or walking from our car to the grocery store, let's open our eyes and praise him with every bird in the sky, leaf on the tree, and stone on the ground.

Father, thank you for creating this beautiful and awe-inspiring world in which I live. I repent of taking for granted my surroundings and failing to give you the honor you deserve. Open my eyes to the wonders around me, both big and small. Teach me to live with a greater awareness of your presence and a heart full of constant praise. I worship your Name and bow before your Glory. In Jesus' name, Amen.

Personal Reflection

Be intentional to notice the beauty in your surroundings today and foster a mindset of constant praise.

_____

_____

_____

_____

_____

_____

_____

_____

_____

_____

_____

_____

_____

Day 55
The Rock

Yesterday we discussed Red Rock Canyon and the praise inherent in God's creation. We'll stay on the topic for one more day to discuss God himself, who is often compared to a rock in Scripture.

Moses, in his final speech to Israel, extolled the attributes of God:

I will proclaim the name of the Lord;
how glorious is our God!
He is the Rock; his deeds are perfect.
Everything he does is just and fair.
He is a faithful God who does no wrong;
how just and upright he is!

Deuteronomy 32:3–4

In describing God as a Rock, Moses proclaimed the steadfastness of God, in which nearly every other attribute of God is rooted. Because God doesn't change, his ways will always be holy and good. Because he is immovable, his justice won't falter, and his love will never end. Because God is strong, he will never fail to protect his children. Because God is stable, he provides a secure foundation on which we can build our lives.

Tragically, those who reject God also experience the justice, strength, and immovability of the Father. Revelation describes a time when the enemies of God hide from his judgment, ironically, among the rocks.

Then everyone—the kings of the earth, the rulers, the generals, the wealthy, the powerful, and every slave and free person—all hid themselves in the caves and among the rocks of the mountains. And they cried to the mountains and the rocks, "Fall on us and hide us from the face of the one who sits on the throne and from the wrath of the Lamb. For the great day of their wrath has come, and who is able to survive?"

Revelation 6:15–17

Those who have rejected God become so terrified of his justice that they pray for the rocks to collapse and crush them. Near the end of their lives, they've finally grasped something of the true nature of God, who is a more powerful force than anything in the natural world.

Although earthly rocks provide a helpful point of reference and help us better understand the Father, even the most awe-inspiring mountain is insignificant in comparison to the reality of God's power. When we worship God with the chorus of creation, we should be mindful of just how infinitely powerful he is. Our Father has the ability to create organisms smaller than the eye can perceive and astral phenomena larger than the brain can conceive. Such awareness should not only deepen our worship but strengthen our faith. The omnipotent, omniscient Father who created the universe will never leave us, forsake us, or stop loving us. Let's stand firm on that foundation today.

Father, thank you for being steadfastly loving, just, and upright. I repent of doubting your goodness and love. Teach me to stand firmly on the foundation of who you are instead of who I am. Help me walk in greater faith and continue to cultivate an attitude of constant praise. Open my eyes to the wonders around me and your work in my world. In Jesus' name, Amen.

Personal Reflection

Continue to be intentional about noticing the beauty in your surroundings today. As you foster a mindset of constant praise, focus especially on the power, strength, and stability of your Father today.

_____

_____

_____

_____

_____

_____

_____

_____

_____

_____

_____

_____

_____

Day 56
Nubian Ibex

Today, I'd like to tell you about the Nubian ibex. Conservation efforts have helped this once endangered species of mountain goat rebound. Found in Asia and Africa, the beautiful creatures are more regal and agile than your average goat.

The ibex thrive in hot, dry climates and can be spotted in mountainous desert terrain. Although their beige colored pelts offer excellent camouflage, the male ibex are striking to behold. Their curved horns, which can grow up to 4 feet long, are used to attract females and defend against predators. The horns are also used to battle one another in competition for available females.

I first became aware of the beautiful creatures while traveling in Israel. Although they are still classified as a "vulnerable" species, they seemed to be everywhere in the Judean Desert. They could be spotted especially along the road-side cliffs and crags. The nimble creatures seemed to defy gravity as they milled about on almost sheer rock faces.

While thrill seekers and adrenaline junkies might find steep cliffs appealing, most of us find them terrifying. Thus, I was anxious simply watching the creatures navigate the steep terrain. I worried they would slip or trip and fall to a horrible death. The ibex themselves, however, were unconcerned by their peril.

I later learned that the hooves of the ibex are uniquely suited for climbing. Cloven and dexterous, the hooves have sharp edges to help them gain traction. The inside of the hooves, however, are rubbery and concave, forming a suction cup that enables ibex to grip the rock securely. In sum, they are perfectly suited to thrive in their environment.

The Psalmist describes God's careful design of animals and their habitats. He even mentions ibex specifically in Psalm 104:18, "The high mountains for the ibex, and rocks a refuge for the hyrax," (my translation). God has likewise equipped us with the gifts, skills, and resources we need to thrive in our environments.

However, we must make sure to ascertain the correct environment and utilize the gifts we've been given. We sometimes wander away from the terrain to which God has called us and wonder why we can't gain traction. Our soul is trying to climb a metaphorical rock face that we were never meant to scale. On the other hand, when we abide in the center of God's will, we can thrive in our purpose and find fulfillment in using the gifts with which we have been blessed. Next time we seem to hit a brick wall, let's pause to reflect. The wall might not represent failure. It might simply be a cliff we were never meant to scale.

Father, thank you for creating me with gifts and skills that will equip me to fulfill my calling. Reveal whether I'm encroaching into any territory to which you have not called me. I ask you to help me discern your will for my life with greater clarity. Lead me to the environment for which you have designed me and empower me to thrive. Help me utilize the resources you've given me for the benefit of your Kingdom. In Jesus' name, Amen.

Personal Reflection

Prayerfully reflect upon your own gifts and skills. Make a list of all the resources with which you have been blessed; write as many as you can think of. Then make a second list that describes your environment—the places, people, and purposes with which you fill your time. Next, consider whether your gifts align with your environment. Do you need to reassess any aspects of your life that might be misaligned with your God-given purpose? Finally, if you have time, read Psalm 104 and thank God for his careful attention to your design.

Scan the QR code for passages of Scripture

Day 56

_____

_____

_____

_____

Day 57
Pottery Shards

During my visits to Israel, much of my time was spent working on the Tel Gezer excavation site. The opportunity to be part of an archaeological dig in the Holy Land was a blessing that I still can't quite wrap my head around. Although the days were hot and the work was grueling, I loved every second of it. Some aspects, however, were quite surprising. You see, Israel is so rich with archaeological artifacts that some of them are simply thrown into junk piles. In particular, pottery shards can be found almost everywhere. One would expect that bronze age pottery, around 3,000 years old, would be valuable even in fragmented form. Nope. Also in our trash pile was a Canaanite ballista ball, which had evidently been launched at the city we were excavating around 3000 years in the past. I was shocked to learn that it, like the pottery, was worthless.

The fascinating, yet worthless, artifacts were a good reminder that material things of this world do not retain value. Although the pottery shards and ballista stone were once valuable—people couldn't exactly run to the store for new ones—today they are nothing more than trash.

Now let's consider our own junk. How many of us have an attic full of things we once found valuable? Or maybe even a whole junk room in our homes? At one time we thought we needed that ab roller, salad spinner, wedding china, and other items that never get used. We go to workday in and day out to earn money for things that soon become worthless and meaningless.

Jesus warns us about placing too much value on perishable things. In John 6:27, he teaches, "But don't be so concerned about perishable things like food. Spend your energy seeking the eternal life that the Son of Man can give you." Our Savior reminds us that no *thing* in this world has eternal value. Anything that isn't from the Father will ultimately deteriorate and rot away. Instead, Jesus calls us to live for him so that our true needs are fulfilled by things that will never perish. He exhorts, "Seek the Kingdom of God above all else, and live righteously, and he will give you everything you need," (Matthew 6:33). If we fix our attention on earthly goods, we will miss out on the best blessings of God. Conversely, if we fix our eyes on God and live for him, we'll be blessed with the best of both worlds. However, we must remember that God's best doesn't always equate to earthly riches, fine dining, fancy houses, and lots of possessions. Remember the old joke—a man wanted to take his gold to heaven, but when he arrived, he found out that all he had was a big load of paving stones. Let's seek what really matters today.

Father, thank you for teaching me to live a life of eternal value. I repent of confusing my wants with my needs. Forgive me for seeking worthless things instead of seeking more of your presence. Forgive me for living for myself instead of living for your Kingdom. Open my spiritual eyes so that I can see that which truly matters in this world. Teach me to forsake materialism in favor of using my resources for your kingdom. In Jesus' name, Amen.

Personal Reflection

Prayerfully consider your financial priorities and spending habits. Do you honor the Lord with your resources or spend freely and without reservation? Do your financial choices reflect a heart that is submitted to God or a desire to live for self? Do you invest in things of eternal value or things that are worldly and perishable? Most likely we are all somewhere in the middle of the spectrum. Ask God to show you one way you can better manage your resources and live for him.

_____

_____

_____

_____

_____

_____

_____

_____

_____

_____

_____

_____

Day 58
Living Water

In a couple of devos near the beginning of the summer, we discussed the importance of consuming God's living water. Over the next few days, we'll discuss impediments to that process as well as strategies for remaining well-hydrated. But first, let me tell you about Ein Gedi.

The largest oasis in Israel, Ein Gedi sits on the border of the Judean wilderness. The beautiful nature preserve boasts one of only two freshwater springs in proximity to the western shore of the Dead Sea. The clean, flowing water nourishes lush vegetation and an abundance of trees such as date palm, apple, fig, and pomegranate. The oasis also serves as a sanctuary for many types of animals such as rabbit, deer, and leopards, as well as ibex, which we discussed yesterday. In addition, well over 200 species of birds reside in the preserve at various points during the year.

Modern-day visitors can enjoy various hiking trails to view the flora, fauna, and stunning waterfalls. A few years ago, I was blessed to visit and hike the "David Waterfall" trail. A short walk, the mostly level pathway leads to a mid-sized waterfall that flows year-round. The shallow basin below the fall holds water that is as clear as crystal. Upon walking through the pool into the spray of the waterfall, I also discovered that it was quite chilly!

I describe the flourishing terrain because I want you to envision the setting. Imagine that you are inhaling the fresh air, feeling the cool spray of the waterfall, hearing the burbling spring, and watching the birds flutter through the trees. The oasis is not only a refuge from the desert, but also a refuge for the soul. In the Edenic setting, God's presence is almost palpable.

It's easy to see why the authors of Scripture refer to such settings as a source of "living water." The constantly flowing stream hydrates the flora and fauna, as well as any humans who seek refuge there. Living water nourishes its surroundings and never grows stagnant, in contrast to saltwater or cistern water.

In fact, when the authors of Scripture refer to living water, they are making a play on words to describe God as a source of life that nourishes and refreshes. In Revelation, Jesus reminds us that we have eternal access to this water. He says, "It is finished! I am the Alpha and the Omega—the Beginning and the End. To anyone who thirsts, I will give freely from the springs of living water," (Rev. 21:6, my translation). Jesus poured himself out when he completed his work on the cross and rose from the dead. We can likewise rise to new life when we accept the living water that he offers. This is both a one-time event in which we decide to follow him, but also a daily process of drinking in his presence. Let's drink deeply today!

Jesus, thank you for pouring yourself out so that I can receive life. I repent of neglecting to spend time in your presence. Cause me to thirst for you more deeply and quench my thirst more regularly. I pray that my spiritual life would flourish like the springs of Ein-Gedi. I ask you to nourish my soul and help me grow into a life-giving oasis for others. In Jesus' name, Amen.

Personal Reflection

Schedule some time today or later this week to spend in God's presence doing something that refreshes your soul and draws you closer to him.

_____

_____

_____

_____

_____

_____

_____

_____

_____

_____

_____

_____

_____

_____

Day 59
Sea Glass

Yesterday, I described the beautiful Ein Gedi oasis in Israel. Another stunning aquatic locale I've visited in Israel is the beach in Ashdod. The beach itself isn't significantly different from those in the Gulf of Mexico, but the crystal-clear Mediterranean water is significantly colder!

Aside from the crisp, clear water, the most striking difference was the seashells. I spent hours combing through the massive quantity of colorful shells that lined the surf. I enjoyed looking at the pretty shells, but I was most excited when I found sea glass. I know sea glass can be found on some beaches in the U.S., but I'd never seen it until that day in Israel. So, as I searched through the shells, I found lovely pieces of blue, green, and amber glass, washed smooth by the sand.

In case you aren't familiar, sea glass begins its journey as a shard of broken glass that somehow makes its way into the ocean. The process of smoothing and shaping can then take 20–40 years, sometimes more. The shards are often used in jewelry and are so beautiful that some artisans create artificial sea glass using a rock tumbler.

Sea glass offers an excellent illustration of spiritual growth. When we begin our walk with God, our souls are riddled with jagged edges and broken pieces. Although God doesn't desire that his children suffer, he knows that trials are the most effective means of sanding down our rough edges and smoothing out our broken areas. So as he keeps us under his watchful eye and in his protective embrace, he allows trials to refine our hearts and minds.

Although the process is often uncomfortable and sometimes painful, our trials increasingly conform us to the image of our Savior. Paul teaches, "And we know that God causes everything to work together for the good of those who love God and are called according to his purpose for them. For God knew his people in advance, and he chose them to become like his Son," (Romans 8:28–29a) God doesn't expect us to enjoy our struggles, but he does call us to trust that he is working everything for our good. As long as we remain in his love and trust in his care, we grow more beautiful every day. Like the sea glass, the process takes many years. In fact, our transformation takes an entire lifetime.

Father, thank you for loving me enough to guide and protect me through trials. In seasons of struggle, help me remember that I am becoming more like my Savior, who also suffered. Help me follow Jesus' pattern of obedience so that I can triumphantly overcome every temptation and trial. I repent of doubting your goodness and love in difficult seasons. Strengthen my soul so that I learn to navigate trials with faith and fortitude. In Jesus' name, Amen.

Personal Reflection

How might God be smoothing and shaping your soul in your current season of life? What trials, struggles, obstacles, or annoyances might God be allowing to refine your soul? Write down 3-5 abrasive areas of life then pray over each and ask God how he might be helping you grow more like Christ in each situation. Write down your thoughts.

Day 60
Fireworks of Fear

My bluebird family typically stays with us all summer long, and we all know what holiday comes right in the middle of the summer—Independence Day. So, one particular 4th of July, our human family gathered on my back patio at dusk to watch the neighborhood fireworks. To say that the bluebirds did not enjoy the sights and sounds would be an understatement. Although the birds had built their nest and prepared for their hatchlings with serenity, the unexpected situation put their lives in turmoil. With each BANG, the poor birds would shoot out of their nest, frantically chirping, flapping, and flying in circles. They would eventually retreat into their home only to be terrified again when the next firecracker exploded. In solidarity with the birds, I became distressed as well, simply because they were so frantic. Yet, I knew that they were safe. The fireworks weren't close enough to hurt them, and they weren't in any real danger.

Through the frenzied behavior of the birds, God showed me that we often respond to trials in a similar fashion. We worry and moan, sometimes cry and sob. Perhaps we obsessively over-prepare, hoard resources, isolate ourselves, or behave destructively. In our own way, we mirror the frantic flapping of the birds, flying in circles and accomplishing nothing.

The Word of God has much to teach us about our response to trials. In Psalm 34:19, we learn that "The righteous person faces many troubles, but the Lord comes to the rescue each time," (Psalm 34:19).

I should note that, unlike the bluebirds, we sometimes face real danger. Jesus specifically tells us, "Here on earth you will have many trials and sorrows," (John 16:33). You and I will face challenges. Period. Jesus wants us to understand that real danger and hardship exist so that when we encounter a trial, we will turn to Him instead of flying into a panic.

You may be in the midst of a trial right now. You may feel like the emotional equivalent of fireworks are exploding all around you. God wants you to understand that he sees you, and he understands your trial. He also wants you to know that he is in complete control and that he has enough strength to deliver you from each fiery ordeal. Let's stop flapping in circles and rest in his strong, loving hands.

Lord, I believe you are strong enough to save me from every trial and keep me from harm. Help me live in the light of your strength and power. Empower me to take captive every thought that does not align with your Word, and help me refrain from any actions that are rooted in a lack of faith. I ask for the strength and wisdom to successfully navigate every situation. Please fill my heart and mind with peace and give me opportunities to share the reason that I can live in peace: Jesus Christ. Amen.

Personal Reflection

Reflect on any trials, difficult situations, or unexpected circumstances in your life. Are these circumstances disrupting your peace of mind and emotional health? Are you responding in counter-productive ways? Ask your Father how you can respond with faith instead of fear. Write your thoughts below.

Day 60

Day 61
Harried Hummingbirds

Summer is the season during which hummingbirds migrate through north Alabama. At first glance, the tiny birds look cute, sweet, and delicate, but if you observe them for any amount of time, you'll see that they are tough and aggressive. I often sit on my back patio watching them battle around the feeder. They routinely dive bomb and peck at each other with their long pointy beaks. They are not, in fact, sweet and delicate at all.

Per usual, I decided to do a little research about hummingbirds to see why they behave so aggressively. I quickly learned that their metabolism is so fast that they have to eat the equivalent of their body weight each day. In fact, they have the highest metabolism of any bird or mammal. Sadly, this high metabolism makes hummingbirds extremely vulnerable to starvation. They constantly live on the edge of survival and can die if they go as little as 3 hours without food. In short, the behavior that I perceived as vicious is just their way of trying to survive.

In a similar manner, we all encounter difficult people from time to time. We might perceive them as rude, pushy, or generally awful to be around. Although I'm not excusing impolite behavior, I think we all need to be reminded that we never know why people behave in certain ways. Those difficult people might be struggling to survive. Your rude co-worker might be dealing with the death of a parent. Maybe that awful lady at the grocery store is experiencing abuse.

Maybe that kid who misbehaves in school doesn't have food to eat at home. We simply don't know what private struggles people are experiencing.

So, how should we respond to those difficult people in our lives? Paul has a wealth of advice, but let me draw your attention to two passages. First, Paul advises, "Don't use foul or abusive language. Let everything you say be good and helpful, so that your words will be an encouragement to those who hear them," (Ephesians 4:29). We might be tempted to return harsh words with a stinging retort, but we would miss a beautiful opportunity to bring encouragement to someone who is hurting. We should daily ask the Holy Spirit to help us refrain from speaking harsh words to or about anyone. Remember the old saying, "If you don't have anything nice to say, don't say anything at all."

Second, Paul encourages us to "Share each other's burdens, and in this way obey the law of Christ," (Galatians 6:2). What is the law of Christ? Jesus told us that the greatest command is to love God and love others (Matthew 22:37). We are called to show others the love of Christ and to bring grace to our world. So, even when we are provoked, even when we don't feel like being kind, even when we are bearing our own burdens, we are called to make an intentional choice to encourage one another. Let's remember that each difficult person we encounter is a beloved son or daughter of Christ and that we have the opportunity to help bear their burdens by showing love, grace, and kindness.

Jesus, thank you for modeling true love and grace through your sacrificial death. Teach me to guard my tongue and hold my temper in heated or difficult situations. I repent of speaking hurtful words to and about people who've angered me. Transform me so that my first instinct is to offer grace and seek reconciliation. Give me the strength to bear the burdens of the people you place in my life. In Jesus' name. Amen.

Personal Reflection

Be especially aware of difficult interactions today. Practice offering grace, speaking kind words, and fostering peace in every situation.

_____

_____

_____

_____

_____

_____

_____

_____

_____

_____

_____

_____

_____

_____

_____

Day 62
Offensive Offerings

July is birthday season in my family. Although my birthday is in December, by some strange coincidence, the bulk of our birthdays fall in July. While I'm not as adept at gift-giving as some, I try to buy presents that are thoughtful, useful, and/or fun.

Imagine, however, if I gave my son a half-eaten birthday cake and a worn-out shirt of his Dad's, or if I gave my mom a potted plant that was half dead. How might they feel? And how would you feel if someone you loved gave you leftovers and trash as a gift?

Sadly, we sometimes approach God with precisely this type of gift. The prophet Malachi records God's message to his people for offering unworthy sacrifices. The Lord begins with the heart wrenching sentiment, "I have always loved you," (Malachi 1:2). Yet despite his love and care, the priests were offering garbage on the altar in the temple. The Lord says,

> *"When you give blind animals as sacrifices, isn't that wrong? And isn't it wrong to offer animals that are crippled and diseased? Try giving gifts like that to your governor, and see how pleased he is!" says the Lord of Heaven's Armies.*
>
> ...
>
> *"But you dishonor my name with your actions. By bringing contemptible food, you are saying it's all*

right to defile the Lord's table. You say, 'It's too hard to serve the Lord,' and you turn up your noses at my commands," says the Lord of Heaven's Armies. "Think of it! Animals that are stolen and crippled and sick are being presented as offerings! Should I accept from you such offerings as these?"

Malachi 1:8, 12–13

God's children were offering sacrifices that blatantly disregarded his statutes and defiled his temple. The people were going through the motions and doing just enough to satisfy appearances.

Although we find their behavior appalling, we often offer sacrifices that are just as unfit. Perhaps we attend worship gatherings only if we have nothing better to do. Perhaps we serve only if we have enough energy remaining at the end of our work week. Perhaps we behave like a Christian only when we are around other Christians. Perhaps we tithe only if we have enough money left at the end of the month.

When we give God our leftovers, we dishonor him as much as the Jewish people who brought him diseased animals. Yet, just as he said to his people nearly 2,500 years ago, he always loves us. Yet, worthless offerings communicate that we don't love him back. When we offer only the dregs of our time, talents, and resources, we reveal that our heart has drifted far from him.

At the root of the issue, God desires that we give heartfelt, sacrificial offerings because he knows that our offerings are an indicator of our spiritual health. God doesn't *need* anything from us—our loving Father wants to give us abundant lives, hearts filled with joy, and purposeful faith. When we open our hands and hearts to him, we are in a position to receive every gift he desires to give.

Father, thank you for showering me with blessings every day. I repent of holding my gifts with clenched fists and giving you leftovers. Give me the courage to surrender every part of my life to you. I pray that you would transform my heart so that my greatest desire is to serve you and use my resources to build your Kingdom. Help me to be a better steward of my time and resources so that I am equipped to give more to you. In Jesus' name, Amen.

Personal Reflection

Meditate on how you manage your time, talents, and financial resources. With which area do you struggle the most? In which area do you tend to give God leftovers? Prayerfully choose one area and then make a plan to better manage that resource and give God your best.

_____

_____

_____

_____

_____

_____

_____

_____

_____

Day 63
Pool Party

Each summer, my family pays for access to the neighborhood swimming pool. When the boys were younger, we visited several times a week. They would play with friends while I laid in the sun and read. The pool was a win-win for us.

As the boys have grown older, we use the pool less frequently. Between their summer jobs and my increased workload, we rarely make it to the pool. We'll likely stop paying for membership next summer, but the thought of losing pool access makes me sad. Even if we don't use it often, I love cooling off by the pool on hot summer days.

But we have to use the pool if we want to enjoy it! I can think about the pool, drive by the pool, and even make tentative plans to visit the pool, but if I never actually get in the pool, I'll never experience the cool, refreshing water.

Similar to my unused pool membership, you and I often neglect God's living water. Our Father wants to offer healing, joy, peace, refreshing, and a multitude of other blessings, but we are simply too busy to stop and drink from his source of life. Like walking past the pool without getting in, we can see what God is doing around us, hear about what Jesus has done, and even attend church, but if we never surrender our lives to Christ and allow him to become our source, we aren't experiencing the abundant life he offers.

The prophet Jeremiah rebuked Judah for abandoning God's living water. He spoke on behalf of God, saying, "For my people have done two evil things: They have abandoned me—the fountain of living water. And they have dug for themselves cracked cisterns that can hold no water at all!" (Jeremiah 2:13). Instead of drinking the living water that was freely offered, God's people toiled in futility. They ignored God's provision and relied upon their own plans, which led to destruction, deportation, and degradation.

We have the opportunity to learn from Judah's mistake, and if we are honest, we've probably experienced some of our own self-induced follies. Yet, when Jesus said "it is finished" on the cross, our Savior referred not only to his own death, which atoned for our sins, but also to his work in restoring our souls and providing an abundant life. Instead of simply having a membership in God's Kingdom, let's jump all the way into Jesus' living water.

Jesus, Thank you for providing the living water that refreshes my soul and empowers me to live an abundant life. I repent of ignoring your presence and going through the motions of being a Christian. I pray that through your Holy Spirit, you would remind me to drink deeply every day. I ask you to refresh my soul and nourish the barren parts of my soul. Help me discern your purpose for my current season of life so that I can walk in it and remain immersed in your will. In your name, Amen.

Personal Reflection

What actions or disciplines are you utilizing to ensure you drink of God's presence regularly? The essentials are prayer, Bible study, worship, and service. If you struggle in any of these four areas, make a plan to integrate them into your routine. If all four are already part of your regular spiritual life, ask God what additional streams of refreshing he might be leading you toward. Write your thoughts below.

Day 64
Hit the Brakes

Unlike me, my son Abel has never been a huge fan of bike riding. It took years for him to learn to ride because, frankly, he didn't want to. We spent days, weeks, and months going in circles around our little cul-de-sac. Eventually, I felt that Abel was ready to venture beyond the safe confines of our street, and we began taking short rides around the neighborhood. Asher and Abel would ride their little-boy bikes and I would jog along beside them in case either of them needed a steadying hand.

I quickly noticed that Abel refused to use the brakes on his bicycle. Whenever he needed to stop, he would simply take his feet off the pedals and use the toes of his shoes as brake pads. Despite my continual coaching and reminders to use the actual brakes, Abel wore the toes off of several pairs of shoes. He simply didn't understand why he needed to use the brakes when his shoes were working perfectly fine.

Sadly, Abel had to learn the importance of bike brakes the hard way. One afternoon, Asher, Abel, and I had decided to go a bit further than usual and tackle a rather large hill. Both boys proudly made it to the top and began to coast down the other side. The boys were single file on the sidewalk with Asher in front and Abel directly behind. As they began to pick up speed, I realized we had a problem. Asher, always cautious, applied his brakes and began to slow himself down. Abel, moving too quickly to apply his shoe-brakes, was barreling closer and closer to Asher. I screamed for Asher to speed up and for

Abel to use his brakes, but neither complied. Abel crashed into Asher and sent himself and his brother skidding across the concrete in a tangle of limbs and bike parts. Thankfully, neither boy had injuries beyond a few scrapes and skinned knees, and both were able to limp home while I awkwardly carried the bikes.

I share this story because the situation highlights an important Scriptural principle. Our Father calls us to learn his ways and obey his commands because he desires to protect us. When we think we know better and go our own way, we invite disaster. Abel thought he had mastered bike riding his own way, but he eventually crashed. And when he crashed, he took another down with him.

The prophet Obadiah outlines the dangers of pride and rebellion. He warns, "The pride of your heart has deceived you—you who live in the clefts of the rock in your lofty dwelling; you who say in your heart, 'Who can bring me down to the ground?'" (Obadiah 3, my translation) If we aren't careful, our pride can deceive us into believing that we are self-sufficient and above harm. However, just as Abel's refusal to heed my advice literally sent him crashing to the ground, our refusal to follow God's principles can turn our lives into a literal wreck. We might not be overtly sinful or rebellious, but neglecting to learn and apply God's Word is just as dangerous. So let's hit the brakes on pride and allow our Father to teach us how to navigate life without a crash and burn.

Father, thank you for providing wisdom for life in your Word. I repent of the pride in my heart and for neglecting your statutes. Forgive me for the times when I knowingly disobeyed you. I ask you to reveal areas of my life in which I'm placing my own prideful will above yours, whether intentionally or unintentionally. Thank you for your commands, which aren't too burdensome or difficult. Enable me to see the benefit of walking in your ways and applying your principles in my life. In Jesus' name, Amen.

Personal Reflection

Prayerfully examine the condition of your heart. Ask God to reveal whether pride has deceived you into going your own way or making bad choices. Consider your finances, relationships, habits, attitudes, and any other area of life that the Lord might bring to mind. Choose one or more situations and for each, write the deceptive lie along with the truth of God with which it needs to be replaced.

_____

_____

_____

_____

_____

_____

_____

_____

_____

_____

_____

_____

_____

_____

Day 65
In the Whirlwind — Part 1

Yesterday we discussed our prideful tendency to navigate life on our own terms. Instead of submitting to God, we often make choices that disregard the clear direction of our Father. Conversely, yet equally disastrous, we often strive to live in obedience, then expect God to reward our righteousness with an easy life. If he doesn't respond to our misguided expectations or answer our prayers the "right" way, we get angry. Or if he allows life to take an undesirable turn, we feel as though he has failed us. At the core, this type of anger, disappointment, and frustration also stems from pride because we think we've earned an optimal outcome for ourselves, our families, and our friends.

In Scripture, Job is a prime example of a righteous person whose life took a disastrous turn for the worse. After losing his livestock, farmhands, and children, "Job did not sin by blaming God," (Job 1:22). Even after his skin erupted into boils from head to toe, Job defended the goodness of God (Job 2:7–13). Yet, as the book proceeds and Job's suffering continues, the man struggles to trust the God who has allowed such tragedy. As Job dialogues with his friends and cries out to the Lord, he wavers between despair, hope, faith, and anger. Some scholars suggest that Job's erratic monologues point to the conflation of different accounts and legends. However, I believe that Job's words expose a heart dealing with excruciating pain, yet fighting to keep the faith.

But I also believe that Job struggled with pride. Toward the end of the narrative, Job cries out,

> *For God has cut my bowstring.*
> *He has humbled me,*
> *so [my enemies] have thrown off all restraint.*
>
> . . .
>
> *I live in terror now.*
> *My honor has blown away in the wind,*
> *and my prosperity has vanished like a cloud.*
> *And now my life seeps away.*
> *Depression haunts my days.*
> *At night my bones are filled with pain,*
> *which gnaws at me relentlessly.*
> *With a strong hand, God grabs my shirt.*
> *He grips me by the collar of my coat.*
> *He has thrown me into the mud.*
> *I'm nothing more than dust and ashes.*
> *I cry to you, O God, but you don't answer.*
> *I stand before you, but you don't even look.*
> *You have become cruel toward me.*
> *You use your power to persecute me.*
> *You throw me into the whirlwind*
> *and destroy me in the storm.*

Job 30:11, 15–22

As Job prays, he accuses the Lord of attacking and persecuting him. He boldly blames God for his misfortune and demands an audience.

The Lord does, indeed, grant an audience and respond to Job. We'll talk about that response tomorrow, but I want to pause today and reflect on a few points. (1) Like David in the Psalms, Job expresses honest thoughts and feelings to God. Our Father knows every emotion in our heart and thought in our head. When we share them, our Father can help us heal. (2) Although he may not fix or erase our problems, God responds when we call out to him.

To anticipate our reading tomorrow, I'll offer three further insights. (3) Our Father doesn't punish or reject us if we become angry with him. He lovingly helps us recognize our flaws and failures so that we can overcome them. (4) As we understand our own shortcomings, God helps us discern the truth of our situation and grow in faith. (5) God is with us in the struggle! Job laments that God has thrown him "into the whirlwind," yet God speaks to Job from within the whirlwind (38:1). Through every tragedy and trial, the Father was near at hand, he heard every prayer, and he responded when the time was right. Today, let's remember that even when God seems far, he might be closer than we can imagine.

Father, thank you for grieving with me when my heart is heavy. Thank you for hearing my prayers and staying close by my side. Help me to trust you even when I don't feel your presence or see your hand at work. Help me trust your goodness even when I see suffering around me. Humble my heart so that I'm not tempted to blame you for evil. Forgive me for valuing my reputation, position, or possessions more than my relationship with you. Give me greater discernment so that I see your loving hand at work in my world and my life. Teach me to lean upon your power rather than trusting in my own strength. In Jesus' name, Amen.

Personal Reflection

Think of a time when you felt so devastated by life that you doubted your faith or God's goodness. Consider how God helped you overcome your trial and heal your heart. What can you learn from that process that might help you navigate future trials with greater faith and fortitude? Or perhaps you are currently in the healing process or in a season of suffering. If so, work through the five points listed above—cry out to God and express your honest thoughts and emotions, ask him to expose any flaws or impediments to healing in your own heart, ask him to help you see with clear eyes of faith, and thank him for staying close by your side.

Day 66
In the Whirlwind — Part 2

The last couple of days we've discussed pride and its relationship to suffering. Yesterday we specifically discussed our tendency to become angry with God when we experience trials. At the core, this type of anger, disappointment, and frustration at God stems from pride. We think we know what should happen to produce an optimal outcome, yet we fail to consider the limited scope of our knowledge and understanding. Today, we'll simply read God's response to Job. I'm keeping my words intentionally brief to allow you more time to read the words of Scripture.

Lord of Hosts, I acknowledge your greatness, power, and knowledge. Teach me to walk in humble reverence of your glory. Help me recognize the limited scope of my own knowledge and abilities. I repent of pride, arrogance, and rebellion. Grow my faith so that my life is characterized by trust and obedience. Give me greater discernment so that I can see your loving hand at work, even from the midst of suffering. Help me trust you even when I don't understand why bad things happen. Thank you for loving me and guiding me. In Jesus' name, Amen.

Personal Reflection

Read Job 38–41. Although the Lord was originally speaking to Job, he is also speaking to you and me. Therefore, read chapters 38–41 as if God were speaking directly to you.

Scan the QR code for passages of Scripture

Day 67
Pride Comes Before the Fall

The last few days we've discussed pride and its impact on our lives and faith. Today, I'd like to look more closely at pride and the reasons why God warns so sternly against it. In the Old Testament, pride is translated from the Hebrew word, *gobah*, which can also refer to height, loftiness, or exaltation. Thus, when we allow pride to take up space in our heart, we are lifting ourselves up and claiming the position that only God deserves. As a result, we place ourselves at odds with our Father.

Pride was the basis of the original sin that separated us from our Lord. From Genesis 3, we learn that,

> *[The woman] saw that the tree was beautiful and its fruit looked delicious, and she wanted the wisdom it would give her. So she took some of the fruit and ate it. Then she gave some to her husband, who was with her, and he ate it, too. At that moment their eyes were opened, and they suddenly felt shame at their nakedness. So they sewed fig leaves together to cover themselves. When the cool evening breezes were blowing, the man and his wife heard the Lord God walking about in the garden. So they hid from the Lord God among the trees.*

> **Genesis 3:6–8**

In their pride, Adam and Eve wanted to access the knowledge of God and take control of their own lives. As a result, they lost their perfect fellowship with God and each other, as well as their absolute peace in his presence. They also ruined the unblemished goodness of God's entire creation. They immediately realized they'd made a horrible mistake, but like squeezing toothpaste out of the tube, prideful sin can't be undone.

Although we would never consciously or purposely demand worship or claim a divine status, we do so unwittingly through our thoughts and actions—each time we look down upon another person or consider someone less important than ourselves, each time we choose to disobey the clear will of our Father, each time we think we are impervious to mistakes or above reproach, each time we speak an unkind word or thoughtless condemnation. Instead of building ourselves up, we are actually ripping the foundation from beneath our lives and hearts.

As we've already discussed, God warns against pride because he is trying to protect us. He isn't worried that we'll usurp his position or become too powerful. He simply knows that pride will destroy us and those we love. Let's resist the temptation to make more of ourselves and give worship only where it is due—to our Heavenly Father.

Father, thank you for covering my prideful sin with your forgiveness and grace. I repent of considering myself better than others. I repent of willful disobedience. I repent of hurtful words and gossip. Empower me to live humbly, speak kindly, and consider others better than myself. Give me a greater desire to build others up than to make myself seem important. Teach me to have the mindset of Christ as I selflessly serve and love your people. In Jesus' name, Amen.

Personal Reflection

Yesterday, you read the Lord's words to Job. Today, read Job's words of repentance to the Lord in Job 42:1–6. After you read, craft your own prayer of repentance and offer it up to the Lord. Be as specific as possible.

Scan the QR code for passages of Scripture

Day 68
Honestly is the Best Policy

The last few days we've discussed the sin of pride and the struggle of Job. Job's anger at the Lord exposed an arrogance in his heart as he accused God of cruelly attacking him. However, Job was an overall righteous man, and I'd like to discuss what he did *right*: Job was honest with God. He railed,

> *Let the day of my birth be erased,*
> *and the night I was conceived.*
> *Let that day be turned to darkness.*
> *Let it be lost even to God on high,*
> *and let no light shine on it.*
> *Let the darkness and utter gloom claim that day for*
> *its own.*
> *Let a black cloud overshadow it,*
> *and let the darkness terrify it.*
> *Let that night be blotted off the calendar,*
> *never again to be counted among the days of the*
> *year,*
> *never again to appear among the months.*
> *Let that night be childless.*
> *Let it have no joy.*

. . .

Oh, why give light to those in misery,
and life to those who are bitter?
They long for death, and it won't come.
They search for death more eagerly than for hidden
treasure.
They're filled with joy when they finally die,
and rejoice when they find the grave.
Why is life given to those with no future,
those God has surrounded with difficulties?

Job 3:3–7, 20–23

Job was brutally honest about how he felt. Although Job's words seem irreverent and even blasphemous at times, he pressed into the Lord rather than pulling away. Job poured his heart out to God, and instead of bottling up his anger and becoming bitter, he directed his complaint to the only One who had the power to do something about it. In doing so, Job positioned himself for restoration and reconciliation. Because he remained close to God, even in his anger, his heart was willing to repent (Job 42:1–6.)

Hear me clearly, I'm not saying that it's good to be angry at God and accuse him of cruelty. What I am saying is that if we feel angry, it's ok to tell God. He already knows, and he is strong enough to handle it. Although God never deserves our anger, expressing our anger to him is much better than walking away from him. If we cling to God through our trials, we'll experience greater growth than we can imagine. So cry and wail all you want, as long as you do it at the feet of Jesus.

Father, I praise you for your infinite power and goodness. I repent of becoming angry and turning away from you when I experience trials. Equip me to turn to you instead of turning to things that will only harm me further. Teach me to offer honest gut-level prayers instead of bland surface-level prayers. Grow my faith and deepen my relationship with you even in my seasons of suffering. Help me remember that you also endured extreme affliction, and that you empathize with my pain. In Jesus' name, Amen.

Personal Reflection

Begin cultivating a deeper and more authentic prayer life in which you converse with God as a dear Friend and trusted Father. Whether or not you are in a season of trial, offer an honest prayer to God today. Share the thoughts and emotions in your heart. Tell him about your hopes and fears. Express your needs and thank him for your blessings. And don't forget to pause and listen for his response.

Day 69
Love Bites

One summer when the boys were in middle school, we traveled to a small exotic zoo. Guests could interact with some of the animals, like the kangaroos, while other animals were cordoned off so that visitors could only view them. The coatimundi was one such species cordoned from the public in a large cage. The playful animals, which look like a mix between a raccoon and a bear, are about the size of a large house cat.

We were enamored with the adorable creatures and longed to pet them. So, despite the posted warning signs, Abel and I proceeded to stick our hands between the bars of the cage. Wesley and Asher looked on with disapproval as we played with the creatures for several minutes. The fun came to a screeching halt, however, when one of the coatimundi bit Abel's hand. The bite wasn't severe enough for stitches, but it bled profusely.

We quickly sought out an employee of the zoo to make sure the animals didn't carry any transmissible diseases. The kind employee reassured us that the animals were healthy and explained that "The coatimundis bite people all the time." We were relieved that the bite wouldn't require a trip to the hospital but frustrated that the zoo hadn't put stronger safeguards in place. We were also embarrassed that we had gotten caught ignoring the warning signs.

Like the widely spaced bars on the coatimundi cage, our Father gives us the freedom to ignore his commands. His statutes are like signs pointing us in the right direction and warning us away from foolish actions. Yet, we are free to go our own way if we so choose. Unfortunately, our own way typically leads to injuries worse than a coatimundi-bitten finger. When we rebel against our Father, we incur damage to our souls, relationships, and bodies.

Our Father gives us guidelines for life because he loves us. But he doesn't force us to obey because he wants us to love him back of our own free will. According to 2 John 6, "And this is love, that we should walk in accordance with his commands; you have heard this command from the beginning so that you could walk in it." When we obey God, we show that we love and trust him. And since loving God is inextricably entwined with loving his people, our obedience also blesses the people in our lives.

To return to the coatimundis, Abel and I created anxiety and inconvenience for Wesley and Asher because we disobeyed the rules. We had to interrupt our enjoyable day to seek help and medical attention. Similarly, our rebellious actions nearly always impact the people in our lives. So, let's trust our Father, obey the signs, and walk in love.

Heavenly Father, thank you for providing guidelines that empower me to live a joyful and purposeful life. I repent of ignoring your commands and disobeying your statutes. Teach me to walk in love and obedience so that I can be a blessing to you and to the people around me. I pray that you would take away any rebellious inclinations and give me a greater desire to walk with you. In Jesus' name, Amen.

Personal Reflection

Prayerfully reflect and ask your Father to reveal whether you are ignoring or disobeying any of his commands in Scripture, whether big or small. Consider whether you are choosing your own desires

Day 69

over submitting to God and obeying him. Write your thoughts below
and then pray for God to grow your love for him to such an extent
that you no longer desire to go your own way.

_____

_____

_____

_____

_____

_____

_____

_____

_____

_____

_____

_____

_____

_____

_____

Day 70
Feedback — Part 1

How do you handle feedback? Constructive criticism can be a hard pill to swallow, but if we hope to become mature Christ-followers, we must learn to choke it down. Allow me to illustrate with a personal experience.

In the early years of my faith (late teens), I was a member of my church's choir and often sang solos in our worship services. We had two services, so anyone singing a solo would sing in each service. One particular Sunday, an older lady approached me after I had sung in the first service. She bluntly told me that my dress was too short, and that I was a stumbling block for other young women. I was utterly crushed. I managed to hold my tears until I could make it into a bathroom stall, where I dissolved into a sobbing mess.

Clearly the feedback was delivered at the wrong time and in the wrong way. I couldn't do anything about my dress before the next service. So, I had to calm down and pull myself together enough to stand in front of the congregation and sing again, feeling like a scarlet letter was emblazoned upon my chest.

Yet, despite the harshness of her criticism and the woman's poor timing, her feedback was valid. My dress was, indeed, too short. So, I swallowed my pride, and from that moment forward made sure to dress more modestly for church. And although I didn't enjoy receiving the feedback, I was thankful for it (after a little time had passed).

Constructive criticism can set us on a healthy path and help us avoid potential obstacles. According to Proverbs 29:1, "Whoever stubbornly refuses to accept criticism will suddenly be destroyed beyond recovery." If we cultivate a habit of ignoring feedback, we set our lives on a trajectory toward destruction. We'll discuss some specifics tomorrow, but let's pause for now to self-reflect.

Father, thank you for placing people in my life who can help me grow. Teach me to receive feedback with maturity and grace. Help me learn even from criticism that is delivered the wrong way. Equip me to be honest with myself and seek the truth rather than making excuses. Give me a desire to continually improve and grow. In Jesus' name, Amen.

Personal Reflection

Prayerfully meditate on your attitude toward feedback and constructive criticism. Do you tend to get defensive or receive correction with grace? Do you allow others to speak into your life or stubbornly go your own way? Write your thoughts below. We'll talk about action steps tomorrow.

_____

_____

_____

_____

_____

_____

_____

_____

_____

_____

_____

_____

_____

_____

_____

_____

_____

_____

_____

_____

_____

_____

_____

_____

_____

Day 71
Feedback — Part 2

Yesterday we began discussing feedback as a tool to become more healthy, mature Christ followers. Today I'll offer a few practical steps that will help us better receive, process, and act upon constructive criticism. Before we delve into action steps, however, let me note that we can learn from all feedback, even that which is unjustified. If we are unfairly attacked, we can learn how to respond with equilibrium, grace, and the peace of our Lord Jesus. We can also learn about the other person and how we should interact with them in the future. For example, might they be speaking out of their own wounds? What type of boundaries might we need to establish with them?

In regard to feedback that is valid, even that which is delivered poorly, you can train yourself to respond productively. First, listen to what is being said. Refrain from making excuses or explaining yourself. Then restate your understanding of the feedback. If your understanding is correct, pause and give yourself time to respond. The more intense your emotional response, the more time you will need to process the feedback. If you are feeling a desire to retaliate in anger or respond with hurtful words of your own, you should ask for more time to consider the feedback before continuing the discussion. Next, prayerfully reflect and seek God's guidance. Ask your Father what he would like you to learn from the interaction. Finally, create an action plan. What do you need to start or stop doing and when? If the feedback was invalid or delivered in a hurtful way, part of your action plan might also involve deciding how you can respond with grace.

As a final note, feedback from a person we deem less than mature or from a person we simply don't like can be even harder than usual to receive. In these cases, we must separate the "who" from the "what." Evaluate the feedback on its own merits rather than dismissing it out of hand. And remember, "Fools think their own way is right, but the wise listen to others," (Proverbs 12:15).

Father, thank you again for placing people in my life who can help me grow. Equip me to learn also from unexpected sources, such as difficult interactions and difficult people. Train me to discern between valid criticism and unfounded attacks. Teach me to respond with the grace and humility of Christ in every interaction. Equip me to be honest with myself and seek the truth rather than making excuses. Give me a desire to continually improve and grow. In Jesus' name, Amen.

Personal Reflection

Seek out a mentor and ask, "What is one thing I can do to improve or grow?" Practice using the steps above to receive, process, and act upon the feedback.

_____

_____

_____

_____

_____

Day 71

Day 72
Out of Africa

I never tire of learning about the lives of biblical figures. I was therefore fascinated when I recently read about the prophet Zephaniah. The first verse of the book that bears his name offers an easy-to-miss tidbit about his heritage. The verse reads, "The Lord gave this message to Zephaniah when Josiah son of Amon was king of Judah. Zephaniah was the son of Cushi, son of Gedaliah, son of Amariah, son of Hezekiah," (Zephaniah 1:1). If you recall, I mentioned in an earlier devotional that genealogies can sometimes be fascinating, and this one doesn't disappoint.

All the names listed in Zephaniah's heritage are standard Jewish fare except for one—Cushi. In Hebrew, Cush is a geographical region that corresponds roughly to Ethiopia. Thus, Zephaniah may have been a multi-racial, black Judean. Old Testament scholar, Jason DeRouchie writes, "Probably Cushi's mother, Gedaliah's wife, was a Cushite, and the parents named their son 'my black one' likely to celebrate his racial heritage."

I should mention that not all scholars agree that Zephaniah was born of a mixed racial heritage. However, I believe that the content of the book offers further support that the prophet was of mixed race. In a beautiful passage the anticipates international peace and racial reconciliation, Zephaniah proclaims,

Then I will purify the speech of all people,
so that everyone can worship the Lord together.
My scattered people who live beyond the rivers of
Cush
will come to present their offerings.
On that day you will no longer need to be ashamed,
for you will no longer be rebels against me.
I will remove all proud and arrogant people from
among you.
There will be no more haughtiness on my holy mountain.
Those who are left will be the lowly and humble,
for it is they who trust in the name of the Lord.

Zephaniah 3:9–12

Zephaniah writes of a future reversal of the Tower of Babel in which linguistic and racial barriers are removed. He describes a time in which peace and humility will replace rebellion and pride, the source of all division.

Christ began the process of restoring all people to God *and* one another. Yet, we await the final consummation of his healing work. In the meantime, we are called to be agents of reconciliation in our world. In a time when race relations are fraught with animosity, we have the opportunity to display the harmonious diversity of God's Kingdom. We must remember that we are more alike than different as we strive to foster unity. In the words of Paul, we "are all one in Christ Jesus," (Galatians 3:28).

Father, thank you for the rich cultural diversity of our world. I pray that you would heal the racial divisions in my country and my world. Help each person, including myself, understand that our differences can become strengths instead of sources of conflict. I ask you to expose any pride or prejudice in my own heart. Give me opportunities to be an agent of reconciliation through my words and actions. In Jesus' name, Amen.

Personal Reflection

First, examine your heart and ask God to reveal any hardened places or unhealed wounds in regard to race relations. Next, ask him if you need to extend forgiveness to someone who has offended you or ask forgiveness of someone you have hurt. Finally, pray for greater empathy toward individuals of other races or cultural backgrounds and begin to seek opportunities for dialogue and mutual growth.

_____

_____

_____

_____

_____

_____

_____

_____

_____

_____

_____

_____

Day 73
Athens Acropolis

In October 2019, just before the world retreated into quarantine, I visited Greece for the first (and only) time in my life. If I'm honest, I was a little disappointed. The cities were dirty and covered in graffiti. Thankfully, the rural areas retained a classic Mediterranean beauty, and the archaeological sites were likewise well-preserved. In particular, the Parthenon, seated upon the Acropolis in Athens, was truly awe-inspiring.

The Parthenon was built in the fifth century B.C. in celebration of the Greek victory over Persian invaders. A temple dedicated to the patron goddess of the city, Athena, the structure also functioned as a city treasury. At different points in history, the temple served as a Christian church and Islamic mosque, not to mention surviving two world wars. One of the most noteworthy buildings in the world, the temple has come to represent the ideals of democracy and Western civilization.

As I stood on the Acropolis and gazed up at the distinctive 2,500-year-old structure, I was amazed by its longevity. It's staggering to think that the Parthenon has outlived the builders and artists who constructed it, as well as centuries of humans who worshiped and worked in it. In the light of such a long and storied history, my life seemed miniscule by comparison.

In reality, our earthly lives are, indeed, short. Yet, our finite existence is not cause for mourning, but an opportunity to grow in wisdom. The Psalmist prays, "Teach us to realize the brevity of life, so that we may grow in wisdom," (Psalm 90:12). In the New Testament, Paul writes similarly "So be careful how you live. Don't live like fools, but like those who are wise. Make the most of every opportunity in these evil days. Don't act thoughtlessly, but understand what the Lord wants you to do," (Ephesians 5:15–17).

When we acknowledge that our days are numbered, we are more likely to make them count. Scripture calls us to acknowledge that we have a finite number of nights to tuck our children into bed, evenings to have dinner with our family, days to accomplish our goals, and moments to share the Gospel.

We often live as if we have all the time in the world, but in fact, we never know how many days, hours, or minutes we have left. This might lead to feelings of anxiety or sadness. However, instead of getting stuck in the doldrums, we should use those emotions as fuel for transformation and growth in wisdom. Let's be encouraged that our Lord is by our side every single day and that he is waiting with open arms when our time on earth is complete. In the meantime, let's make every moment count!

Lord, thank you for giving me a life of meaning and purpose. Help me discern your will for my life in this season. Teach me to live thoughtfully and make the most of every opportunity. Help me steward my time well so that I accomplish your plans for my life. Give me the capacity to make wise decisions that lead to meaning and fulfillment. Equip me to invest in eternal treasures rather than temporary pleasures during my time on this earth. In Jesus' name, Amen.

Personal Reflection

Consider the finitude of your own life. How can you better steward your time and make each day count? Write your thoughts below. In addition, be intentional to live purposefully, express love, and share encouragement TODAY!

_____

_____

_____

_____

_____

_____

_____

_____

_____

_____

_____

_____

_____

Day 74

Leaving a Legacy

Yesterday, we discussed the wisdom in being mindful of life's brevity. As we ponder the span of our life on this earth, we often think about the legacy we will leave behind. I'm sure we all hope to leave a positive legacy, but we can do more than just hope. We can be intentional to equip and prepare those who will follow after us.

In Scripture, David models this principle by leaving an astounding legacy for his son, Solomon. Although David wasn't perfect, he modeled a life of faith and perseverance. He also left a tangible legacy so that Solomon could successfully fulfill God's purpose for his own life. Before he died, David summoned all the leaders of Israel and publicly commissioned Solomon to build the temple. According to 1 Chronicles 28,

> *David rose to his feet and said: "My brothers and my people! It was my desire to build a Temple where the Ark of the Lord's Covenant, God's footstool, could rest permanently. I made the necessary preparations for building it, but God said to me, 'You must not build a Temple to honor my name, for you are a warrior and have shed much blood.' . . . He said to me, 'Your son Solomon will build my Temple and its courtyards, for I have chosen him as my son, and I will be his father. And if he continues to obey my commands*

251

and regulations as he does now, I will make his Kingdom last forever.' So now, with God as our witness, and in the sight of all Israel—the Lord's assembly— I give you this charge. Be careful to obey all the commands of the Lord your God, so that you may continue to possess this good land and leave it to your children as a permanent inheritance. And Solomon, my son, learn to know the God of your ancestors intimately. Worship and serve him with your whole heart and a willing mind. For the Lord sees every heart and knows every plan and thought. If you seek him, you will find him. But if you forsake him, he will reject you forever. So take this seriously. The Lord has chosen you to build a Temple as his sanctuary. Be strong, and do the work."

1 Chronicles 28:2–3, 6–10

David exhorted Solomon to remain faithful to God so Solomon would himself be equipped to leave a legacy for his children. But David gave his son much more than encouraging words. The king drafted plans for the temple, its implements, and its courtyards. He provided instructions for the priestly roles and responsibilities. He contributed gold, costly metals, and precious jewels to adorn and finance the project. He even appointed seasoned advisors to guide Solomon (1 Chronicles 28:11–29:9).

David set an almost impossibly high standard with his legacy, and although he was a man after God's own heart, he was still just a man. His example of planning and preparation should inspire us to set big goals and high standards for ourselves. David's legacy was the work of a lifetime, and his work reveals that it's never too early to begin.

Whether we are called to leave a financial legacy, a spiritual legacy, a relational legacy, or something altogether different, we can start laying the foundation today.

Father, thank you for family members, mentors, and friends whose legacies have impacted my life. Empower me likewise to leave a legacy of faith and love. Forgive me for wasting my time and resources on meaningless pursuits. Show me how I can take practical steps to leave a tangible legacy that has a lasting impact on your Kingdom. Teach me to steward my resources well so that I'm able to equip others to serve you well and accomplish your plans for their lives. In Jesus' name, Amen.

Personal Reflection

Prayerfully meditate on your own legacy. What type of lasting impact do you hope and pray for? Write down your thoughts, then determine a few intentional and practical steps you can take to bring your legacy to fruition.

_____

_____

_____

_____

_____

_____

_____

Day 74

Day 75
Hungry Baby

One summer when my husband was a little boy, he happened upon a baby bird while walking through the woods with a friend. The bird had seemingly fallen from its nest and been abandoned by its mother. Having compassion on the poor creature, Wesley and his friend decided to feed the baby bird. They trekked to a nearby stream in search of food and located an ample supply of tadpoles. The boys, thus, gathered several of the tiny swimmers for the bird. Fearing that the hatchling would choke on the tadpoles, they mashed them up for easy digestion. The little bird hungrily consumed its meal, and the boys departed with plans to check on it later.

The next day, Wesley and his friend returned to find that the meal of tadpoles hadn't digested well at all. Sadly, the baby bird had thrown everything up. Fearing that they would harm the bird if they tried to help further, they left the hatchling to its own devices and hoped that its mother might return.

I'll never know what happened to that hungry baby bird, but I do know that you and I have a very real spiritual hunger. We were designed to receive daily nourishment from our Heavenly Father. Moses taught, "People do not live by bread alone; rather, we live by every word that comes from the mouth of the Lord," (Deuteronomy 8:3b).

When Jesus fasted in the desert, he rebuked the Enemy with those same words. Matthew records,

> *Then Jesus was led by the Spirit into the wilderness to be tempted there by the devil. For forty days and forty nights he fasted and became very hungry. During that time the devil came and said to him, "If you are the Son of God, tell these stones to become loaves of bread." But Jesus told him, "No! The Scriptures say, 'People do not live by bread alone, but by every word that comes from the mouth of God.'"*

Matthew 4:1–4

Jesus could have eaten food anytime he desired, but he knew that true spiritual nourishment from the Father is more life-giving than any earthly cuisine.

You and I are like hungry little baby birds. We have a deep seeded hunger, but we don't always have the discernment to partake of nourishing and healthy fare. We simply open our mouths and consume whatever culture shoves in our face. The results can be disastrous as the Enemy steals our emotional, physical, and mental health, then destroys our relationships and our purpose. Instead, we should be training ourselves to consume fare that nourishes our minds, bodies, and souls. Peter admonishes, "So get rid of all evil behavior. Be done with all deceit, hypocrisy, jealousy, and all unkind speech. Like newborn babies, you must crave pure spiritual milk so that you will grow into a full experience of salvation. Cry out for this nourishment, now that you have had a taste of the Lord's kindness," (1 Peter 2:1–3).

Father, thank you for nourishing my soul and my body. Forgive me for trying to satiate my hunger on things of this world instead of your presence. Give me a desire for you that surpasses everything this world has to offer. Help me rid my heart of evil behaviors, deceit, hypocrisy, jealousy, unkind speech, and any other type of thought or behavior that dishonors you. Teach me to discern the difference between fare that will nourish me and trash that will poison my soul. I desire to experience your salvation to the fullest. In Jesus' name, Amen.

Personal Reflection

Prayerfully consider what you are feeding your soul. Are God and his Word your primary sources of nourishment or do you seek fulfillment in temporary pleasures? Review your notes from days 7–9. Are you continuing to cultivate habits that equip you to "grow into a full experience of salvation"? Assess your progress and determine any areas in which you might need to course correct.

_____

_____

_____

_____

_____

_____

_____

_____

_____

_____

_____

_____

Day 75

_____

_____

_____

_____

_____

_____

_____

_____

_____

_____

_____

_____

_____

_____

_____

_____

Day 76
Spanish Moss

In a couple of winter devotionals, we discussed mistletoe, an arboreal plant that draws nutrition from host trees. Today I would like to tell you about another arboreal plant found throughout the deep South—Spanish moss. The curly, thin strands grow upon the branches of large trees in humid, swampy regions. Most often found on southern live oaks, the moss drapes itself across the twisting branches like beautiful, silvery hair. If you've ever walked beneath such trees, you know that the moss creates an enchanting, ethereal atmosphere.

Until recently, I'd never realized that Spanish moss was a living plant. In fact, it's classified as an epiphyte, which means that it draws moisture and nutrients from the air. Unlike other tree-dwelling, parasitic plants like mistletoe, Spanish moss draws no nourishment from its host trees.

As usual, learning about the moss made me love it even more. So, newly fascinated with the plant, I brought home a large bundle after my most recent trip to New Orleans. Once home, I distributed the moss among various other plants and containers, and I continued to meditate upon its properties. I felt the Lord nudge my spirit with the question, "What if my people took responsibility for their own growth instead of depending upon others to feed them?" Like the Spanish moss, God calls us to take responsibility for our own health and growth.

As a Bible teacher, my heart is often grieved by the seeming lack of interest many of God's people have toward his Word. Even if we attend church every Sunday, we'll receive only two hours of biblical teaching per *month*. Instead, our Father calls us to nourish ourselves daily upon his Word.

The Psalmist describes the joy and security derived from a personal devotion to studying God's statutes. He rejoices,

Oh, how I love your instructions!
I think about them all day long.
Your commands make me wiser than my enemies,
for they are my constant guide.
Yes, I have more insight than my teachers,
for I am always thinking of your laws.
I am even wiser than my elders,
for I have kept your commandments.
I have refused to walk on any evil path,
so that I may remain obedient to your word.
I haven't turned away from your regulations,
for you have taught me well.
How sweet your words taste to me;
they are sweeter than honey.
Your commandments give me understanding;
no wonder I hate every false way of life.

Psalm 119:97–104

The Psalmist didn't depend upon his teachers to spoon-feed him God's Word. In fact, he studied so diligently that he surpassed his elders in wisdom. He was transformed as he learned the ways of God and began to walk in them. His intimacy with the Lord empowered him to recognize deception, avoid evil, and seize each day with joy.

If you are reading these devotionals, I know you already hunger for God's Word. I encourage you to stoke that desire and continue growing in maturity by searching the Scriptures for yourself.

Lord, thank you for the gift of Scripture. I ask you to grow my desire to spend time in study, and I repent of neglecting time in your Word. Help me prioritize my studies rather than allowing other parts of my life to get in the way. Give me understanding and clarity as I seek to learn your statutes. I ask for a greater knowledge so that I can remain on your path and avoid evil ways. In Jesus' name, Amen.

Personal Reflection

Re-read Psalm 119:97–104 above. Underline every benefit of God's Word, then read the passage again and circle every action the Psalmist takes to receive these benefits. Compare and contrast your own attitudes and habits with those of the Psalmist, and write your thoughts below.

_____

_____

_____

_____

_____

_____

_____

Day 76

Day 77
Dead Bugs

My younger son Abel is endlessly fascinated by the world around him. He especially enjoys discovering the strange and unusual. I've already mentioned our beach explorations, during which he spends hours upon hours searching for interesting aquatic creatures. He also loves searching for unusual flora and fauna on dry land.

One particular summer, Abel decided to start an insect collection. He carefully captured bees, flies, moths, and whatever else he found intriguing. He then placed each insect in a plastic bag for observation. Of course, the insects soon died, after which, he stored them in his dresser drawer. I was aware of his project, and I found it somewhat gross, but I didn't see any reason to impede his exploration. I certainly didn't want to stifle his curiosity, and I figured the hobby was more worthwhile than video games.

The problem arose after a few weeks passed. Not surprisingly, the dead bugs started to smell. And after a while, the smell passed right through the plastic baggies. Since they were still contained inside the dresser, the stench continued to build until it finally escaped the drawer in which it was held. Upon noticing the odd smell and opening Abel's dresser, I was met with one of the most nauseating, putrid scents I've ever experienced. It was so awful that Abel didn't hesitate when I told him to get rid of the bugs and clean the dresser immediately.

When I think of the decomposing bug collection, I think of the way bitterness works in our lives. It often begins with a small offense, unmet expectation, or angry thought. We feel justified in holding onto our hurt or hoping for vengeance. Yet, as we keep our wound stored in our heart, our mental and emotional state slowly begins to deteriorate such that we begin to collect more offenses. Eventually, our collection of hurts begins to fester and stink.

The author of Hebrews cautions us to remain on guard so that no root of bitterness can begin to grow in our hearts. He teaches, "Watch out that no poisonous root of bitterness grows up to trouble you, corrupting many," (Hebrews 12:15b). When we allow bitterness to grow in our heart, we not only corrupt our own lives, but the lives of people around us. Like the stink wafting from Abel's dresser, the odor of our bitterness spreads decay and strife everywhere. And the longer we allow our bitterness to fester, the more rotten it becomes. Let's clean any old, stinking offenses from our hearts today!

Jesus, thank you for teaching me to forgive and for modeling forgiveness during your earthly life. Help me to let go of any hurts before they have time to take root and fester. Forgive me for harboring unforgiveness in my heart and for causing others to stumble when my bitterness shows through. Empower and equip me to release every unmet expectation, angry thought, or unforgiven offense to you. Give me the mental and spiritual discipline to trust you to be my defender and protector. In Jesus' name, Amen.

Personal Reflection

Prayerfully meditate on any "bitter roots" you might be harboring in your heart. Write them below, then pray over your list and release each one to God. Make a decision to release each offense to God as many times as needed and decide to entrust him with the outcome. Ask God to heal your heart if your emotions don't yet align with your faith-filled decision.

_____

_____

_____

_____

_____

_____

_____

_____

_____

_____

_____

_____

_____

_____

_____

Day 78
Be a Bee

In recent years, we've become increasingly aware of the vital role that bees play in our ecosystem. They can be found in nearly every plant-bearing habitat and on every continent except Antarctica. Bees are essential for the pollination of flowers and food-bearing crops. They are responsible for the fruits and vegetables we eat as well as the grains upon which our livestock feeds. And let's not forget honey, which is delicious, nutritious, and antibacterial! Bees are so vital to our planet that they are considered a keystone species, one upon which the entire ecosystem depends.

As I've read about bees, I've been fascinated to learn that scientists believe modern bees evolved from predatory wasps. These various wasp species not only prey on fellow insects for food, but parasitically lay their eggs inside other insects, who are consumed from the inside-out. Yet other species of wasp create small nests for their larvae and retrieve insects for their young, much like birds and their hatchlings. Researchers believe that bees emerged from this nesting type of wasp, as the wasps gradually began feeding their grubs pollen instead of other insects.

Although the wasps and bees are simply acting upon instinct, I can't help but imagine that the wasps are angry and vengeful while the bees are happy and kind. I envision the wasps attacking fellow creatures with malice while the bees are spreading joy and nourishing the world around them. And if you'll allow me to extend my imaginings, you and I can choose to be a wasp or a bee. When we experience anger, we can become vengeful, lashing out at others and seeking to eradicate their joy. Or we can choose to trust God, move on to the next flower, and nourish the world with our compassion and joy.

David exhorts us to turn away from our anger and turn to our Father. He writes,

> *Be still in the presence of the Lord,*
> *and wait patiently for him to act.*
> *Don't worry about evil people who prosper*
> *or fret about their wicked schemes.*
>
> *Stop being angry!*
> *Turn from your rage!*
> *Do not lose your temper—*
> *it only leads to harm.*
>
> ### *Psalm 37:7–8*

We don't need to indulge our anger or seek revenge. As we discussed yesterday, anger can turn into a root of bitterness that destroys our lives from within and without. But David reminds us that God is our defender. Our Father is big enough and strong enough to fight on our behalf. We must choose to focus on him rather than focusing on our offense. We might still *feel* angry, but we can choose not to allow our anger to control us. Let's resolve to be a honeybee instead of a nasty wasp.

Father, thank you for being my defender—for going before me, guarding my back, and protecting me on every side. Teach me to rest in your presence and keep my gaze upon you. Train me to entrust my hurts and offenses to you rather than seeking vengeance or retribution. I repent of seeking revenge and harboring unforgiveness. Fill my heart with such love that there is no room for a root of bitterness to grow. Empower me to extend grace and compassion to others just as you have extended your love to me. In Jesus' name, Amen.

Personal Reflection

Review your notes from yesterday, pray over your list of "bitter roots" and again release each one to God. Next, prayerfully assess how you manage moments of anger throughout your day. Do you lose your temper and react strongly or do you seek God's presence and respond with grace. Be conscious of your interactions today and practice seeking God's presence in frustrating moments instead of letting your emotions control you.

_____

_____

_____

_____

_____

_____

_____

_____

_____

_____

_____

Day 79
Seedy Faith

A delightful feature of late summer is the impatiens seed pods. We fondly refer to them as "poppers" because when the boys were little, they loved to watch them pop. Basically, once a flower grows to maturity and falls away, it leaves behind a tiny seed pod that grows larger and larger until it explodes. If you catch them at just the right moment, you can give the pod a gentle touch and watch it launch seeds into the air. And believe me — they go everywhere! Each year, I look forward to seeing where new impatiens emerge from the ground. They've even mysteriously sprouted from several houseplants.

I think the impatiens' seeds are an excellent analogy for our call to spread the Gospel. As we grow in maturity and sanctification, God prepares us to plant seeds and produce fruit. In fact, we have a direct commission to "go and make disciples of all the nations," (Matthew 28:19a). Jesus teaches, "You didn't choose me. I chose you. I appointed you to go and produce lasting fruit," (John 15:16a). Further, "when you produce much fruit, you are my true disciples. This brings great glory to my Father," (John 15:8). Since our very purpose in life is to glorify God, we should be intentional to sow seeds and bear fruit on his behalf.

Like my impatiens, we are all planted in different places. We are planted in different cities and different professions. We are proximate to different people and cultures, and we each have different opportunities to share the love of Christ. Our process of planting seeds might look very different. Some people and places might be so resistant to the Gospel that our ministry is simply kindness. Alternately, we might be planted in a professional setting in which we aren't allowed to share the Gospel. Nonetheless, we all have an opportunity to show God's love through our actions, even if we can't share directly.

When we are diligent to plant seeds, we will reap a harvest, without fail. Like my impatiens, we don't know when or where new growth will occur. But as we glorify our Father, our words and actions are never futile.

Jesus, thank you for showing me how to plant the seeds of God's Kingdom. Teach me to discern when to speak and when to remain silent, when to take action and when to restrain myself, when to show love and when to offer correction. Help me be more sensitive to your guidance through the Holy Spirit. Forgive me for failing to take advantage of every opportunity to spread the Gospel. Help me see all people through your eyes and be moved by compassion to share your love with them. In Jesus' name, Amen.

Personal Reflection

Look for opportunities to plant seeds of the Gospel today. Be bold and challenge yourself to share God's love in a new way.

_____

_____

_____

_____

_____

_____

Day 79

Day 80
Moonflowers

Among the most interesting plants I grow each year are my moonflower vines. You might deduce from the name that the flowers on this vine open at night. During the day, the blossoms are curled into tight cylinders, but as dusk falls, the blooms unfurl into lovely white flowers. The process happens slowly, with the flowers opening fully only when the sky is completely dark. I enjoy watching the process, but even more so, I relish trying to capture a perfect time-lapse video at least once a summer.

The unique nature and timing of the moonflower always makes me think about the way God gifts his children. Each of us has a unique manner in which we are called to serve the Lord. Now, we *all* are called to lives of faith, hope, love, and service, but God also has a specific plan for each of us. Further, the timing and pace of our calling may look very different from that of our peers.

Let's look at the Levites, for example. In 1 Chronicles, we learn about the myriad of responsibilities held by this tribe. Although Levi was the priestly tribe, not all Levites were priests. Some were gatekeepers of the temple, and some were musicians (1 Chronicles 9:17–27, 33).

> *[Others] were assigned to care for the various articles used in worship. They checked them in and out to avoid any loss. Others were responsible for the furnishings, the items in the sanctuary, and the supplies,*

such as choice flour, wine, olive oil, frankincense, and spices. But it was the priests who blended the spices. Mattithiah, a Levite and the oldest son of Shallum the Korahite, was entrusted with baking the bread used in the offerings. And some members of the clan of Kohath were in charge of preparing the bread to be set on the table each Sabbath day.

1 Chronicles 9:28–32

We might be tempted to think the gatekeepers, bakers, and other Levites were less important than the men who served as priests. Perhaps the men with more mundane duties were even a bit jealous of their priestly brethren. Yet, the Korahites, mentioned in the passage above, are associated with Psalm 84, "A Psalm of the Sons of Korah," in which the psalmist writes, "I would rather be a gatekeeper in the house of my God than live the good life in the homes of the wicked," (Psalm 84:10b). Every task done in the service of the Father is worthy of honor. Comparison has no place in his Kingdom.

Do you compare yourself to others as you seek to live out God's plan for your life? Perhaps you feel that your career is moving too slowly or that your spiritual gifts aren't being utilized in your church. Perhaps you are looking for a spouse but can't seem to find the right mate. Perhaps you are longing for children but struggling to conceive. Perhaps you are looking at everyone around you, wondering why you seem to be stuck in place, lacking meaningful momentum.

If you start to feel inadequate, defeated, or worthless, remember the moonflower. The pace of your life is the pace of *your* life, and no one else's. God will bring growth and flowering at just the right time and just the right pace. If you are expecting your life to look like that of your peers, consider that God might have a different calling for you. Your gifts, skills, and calling are your own, not to be compared or measured against anyone else's. Let's lean into God, rejoice in the gifts he has given us, and be the best darn doorkeepers in the temple and moonflowers in the garden.

Father, thank you for creating me with value and purpose. I repent of basing my self-worth on external factors like success or notoriety. I repent of comparing myself to others instead of finding meaning in your plans for me. Help me root my significance and identity in you alone. Teach me to find joy even in mundane or insignificant tasks when they are done in your service. Guide me as I seek to discover my calling and walk in it. Give me the patience to wait on your timing and trust your pace. In Jesus' name, Amen.

Personal Reflection

Prayerfully reflect on your attitude toward success and significance. Do you locate your worth in God alone or do you seek value by comparing yourself to others? Do you eschew mundane acts of service in favor of tasks that seem more important or visible? Write your thoughts below and pray for a humble heart that reflects that of our Savior, Jesus.

_____

_____

_____

_____

_____

_____

Day 80

Day 81
When We All Get to Heaven?

Heaven has long been the ultimate goal and hope of every Christian. We barely need to glance through traditional hymnals to encounter lines such as "In the mansions bright and blessed, He'll prepare for us a place. When we all get to heaven, what a day of rejoicing that will be!"

But how do *you* picture "heaven"? What pops into your mind when you imagine the place in which we'll spend eternity with God? Most of us can't help but envision an otherworldly paradise in the clouds, possibly filled with gold streets, bejeweled architecture, and lavish mansions, perhaps also inhabited by beautiful angels playing harps. We've already discussed angels in a winter devotional, and in case you haven't read it, angelic beings are more akin to frightening warriors than gentle harp-players. Likewise, the biblical portrayal of heaven bears little resemblance to the imaginary cloud paradise often found in paintings and movies.

Despite our focus on heaven in the modern church, Scripture has shockingly little to say about the afterlife. The Old Testament authors make no mention of "heaven" except in reference to the place where God lives or to the literal heavens, i.e., the sky. They certainly offer no indication that we will go to "heaven" when we die. The New Testament authors use the term similarly, while also making frequent references to the Kingdom of Heaven. Rather than a place we go upon death, however, believers are already part of this Kingdom. Biblical authors only mention *going to* heaven in a couple of brief (and often confusing) verses. Heaven was simply not a matter of great concern to biblical authors. The fathers of our faith were much more interested in how we live today than where we go when we die. Further, they envision an eventual restoration of God's good creation, not a departure from it when we die.

John 14 is a passage often cited to promote the idea of an otherworldly heaven, in which we dwell in lavish mansions for eternity. In John 14:2–3, Jesus says to his disciples, "In my Father's house there are many rooms; unless it were so, would I say to you that I go to prepare a place for you? And if I should go and prepare a place for you, I will come again and receive you to myself, that where I am also you will be," (my translation). Although we don't have the time or space here for a detailed theological discussion, I'd like to offer a few key points to help you understand the passage more accurately.

First, "the Father's house" is a clear reference to the Jerusalem temple (John 2:16). Until Christ, the temple was the primary means by which God fulfilled his covenant promise to dwell among his people. Upon the advent of Christ, Jesus himself replaced the temple as God's presence incarnate (John 2:16–21). Through Christ, you and I have direct access to the Father, even more so than the Jewish priests who ministered in the temple.

Second, the "many rooms" aren't rooms at all. The Greek term for "rooms," *mone*, is rare and was mistranslated into the Latin Scriptures as *mansiones*, which was intended to convey stations or resting places along the soul's journey to heaven, which in itself, has no Scriptural basis. Then, unfortunately, many modern translators rendered the Latin term literally into English as "mansions." However, the root of the term is often used in the Gospel of John to reference remaining or abiding in the presence of Jesus and the Father. Case in point, in John 14:23 Jesus says, "All who love me will do what I say. My Father will love them, and we will come and make our home (*mone*) with each of them."

Third, just as the rooms aren't rooms, the "prepared place" isn't a literal spatial location. The language of a "prepared place" resonates with theological significance. Variously used to describe the promised land, the temple, and the very presence of God, the "prepared place" is the culmination of God's promises to his people.

In the light of such usages, the evolution of the phrase might be considered complete in regarding Jesus as the Messiah who "prepares" the "place," i.e., the crucifixion and resurrection of his own body. In conjunction with "my Father's house," the phrase reveals a concern to reconceive temple imagery as the new household of God—the community of believers, abiding in the presence of Christ and the Father.

So, are you hanging in there? If you feel a little foggy, that's perfectly normal. We'll talk more on the topic tomorrow, but for today, I simply want you to reassess your ideas of heaven. Heaven is real—it just might not look like we think.

Father, thank you for making your presence available to me through Christ. Help me to abide in your presence today rather than placing my hope in a future paradise. Forgive me for relying on my faith simply as a way to avoid hell and get into heaven. Teach me to read the Bible for myself, to prioritize what you prioritize, and to understand the truth of Scripture. In Jesus' name, Amen.

Personal Reflection

Write down your expectations regarding heaven. What do you think it will look like and feel like? Who will be there and what will you do?

Day 81

Day 82
Walk This Way

Yesterday I challenged you to reassess your ideas about heaven, and we began examining John 14:2–3. Today I would like to continue working through the passage. In verse 3, Jesus says, "And if I should go and prepare a place for you, I will come again and receive you to myself, that where I am also you will be," (John 14:3, my translation). As I suggested yesterday, I don't believe the prepared "place" is a place at all, but the process of Jesus' death and resurrection, by which he prepares the way for us to enter the presence of the Father. But, if Jesus isn't going to heaven to prepare our mansions, where is he going?

The Greek verb used to describe Jesus' "going" is *poreuomai*. In the spatial sense, the term indicates movement from one place to another, as in walking or journeying. Yet, the verb also has a well-attested moral sense, as in living for Christ or walking with the Lord, idioms that remain common today. The expression originates in the Old Testament from the Hebrew equivalent of the term for walking, *halak*. The moral sense of the term is found often in passages such as Psalm 86:11, "Teach me, God, your way, and I will *walk* in your truth," (translation and italics mine). The moral connotation is also reflected in New Testament verses such as Luke 1:6: "And [Zechariah and Elizabeth] were both righteous in the presence of God, *walking* blamelessly in all the commands and requirements of the Lord," (translation and italics mins).

In the light of ethical overtones inherent in the idea of "going," I believe that Jesus' words in 14:2b might be interpreted more accurately as, "For I go to the Cross to enable you to abide in the presence of God." Along such lines Jesus' "going" not only reconciles believers with the Father but provides the perfect model of obedience.

To continue working through John 14:3, after Jesus "goes," he promises to return. He says, "I will come again and receive you to myself, that where I am also you will be," (John 14:3b). The phrase is often understood as Jesus' promise to return to earth, gather his followers, and transport them to heaven. However, a close examination of the text reveals that Jesus does not promise to take his followers anywhere at all, other than "to himself." In fact, the phrase bears even greater depth of meaning when understood as believers receiving the immediate, personal presence of Jesus as opposed to a roomy, ethereal dwelling place.

The following verse, John 14:4, supports a relational understanding of the phrase. Jesus says, "And you know the way where I go," (my translation). Here, Jesus never explicitly states that the disciples know *where* he is going, only the *way*. Indeed, the way is not an indicator of direction, but a commitment to follow Christ, in line with going/walking in 14:2. Jesus does not point the way, he *is* the way, as he explains in verse 6, "I am the way, the truth, and the life. No one can come to the Father except through me," (John 14:6).

So, how does all this impact our life and faith? If we narrow the experience of salvation to escaping hell and going to heaven, we miss the life-changing beauty and power of the Gospel. If we understand that we enter the Kingdom of Heaven the moment we accept Christ, we begin to realize that the most important aspect of "heaven" is the presence of God himself, which we have access to *right now!* As we abide in his presence and walk in his ways, we are increasingly transformed by our Savior. In the process, we become agents of redemption and change in our world. So even as we look forward to eternity with God one day in the future, let's choose to walk in the ways of Christ each day and start seeking heaven right now!

Jesus, thank you for walking in obedience to the point of death and making a way for me to abide in the presence of my Father. Help me emulate your life of faith as I walk with God. Teach me to focus on the eternal impact of my words and actions today and every day. Teach me to search the Scriptures without preconceptions and to receive whatsoever you would reveal to me. Empower me to usher your Kingdom to this earth as I spread the good news of the Gospel message. In your name, Amen.

Personal Reflection

Yesterday you wrote down your expectations regarding heaven. Today ask God to help you reassess your expectations in the light of Scripture. Are you willing to let go of any ideas that might be inconsistent with his Word? If you have time, use your concordance to look up and read several verses about heaven from the Old Testament and New Testament. Jot down what you learn.

_____

_____

_____

_____

_____

_____

Day 82

Day 83
Heaven on Earth

The last couple of days we've discussed heaven and looked closely at Christ's message in John 14:2–4. Although John 14 is often read as a passage about "going to heaven," Jesus gives no indication that he will transport his followers to an otherworldly dwelling. When Jesus receives believers to himself, he is drawing them into the presence of the Father, not transporting them to another realm. Rather than promising an ethereal paradise, Jesus urges his followers to emulate his pattern of obedience in order to foster deeper fellowship with the Father. Jesus' departure, rather than creating separation, provides greater access to God. The death of Jesus is the preparatory act that makes mutual indwelling between God and believers possible. In his going away, Jesus provides the perfect model of obedience, while at the same time reconciling believers to God through his sacrifice.

But if heaven isn't an otherworldly home to which we go when we die, what is it and where is it? As I hinted yesterday, we are already part of the Kingdom of Heaven, which isn't a place, but a people. When we accept Christ, we become part of his Kingdom and receive a place in his presence for eternity. So the extent to which we dwell in his presence and walk with the Lord is the extent to which we experience heaven right now! As we seek to transform our world through the power of the Gospel, we foreshadow a more complete and final restoration that Christ will consummate when he returns.

So, in short, heaven is right here on earth! In Revelation 21, God comes to dwell among his people, uniting his dwelling space and our dwelling space for eternity. John records,

> *And I saw a new heaven and a new earth. For the first heaven and the first earth passed away, and the sea was no more. I saw the holy city, the New Jerusalem, descending from heaven from God, having been prepared, adorned as a bride for her husband. And I heard a loud voice from the throne, saying, "Behold, the dwelling of God among humanity! He will dwell with them, and they will be his people. God himself will be with them, as their God. He will wipe away every tear from their eyes, and death will be no more. Neither will there be mourning, nor crying, nor pain. For the first things have passed away." And the one sitting on the throne said, "Behold, I am making all things new!"*

Revelation 21:1–5a (my translation)

After the new heaven and earth descends, John describes a new Eden in which creation is healed. All nations dwell in God's presence, walk in his light, and worship his Name.

The arc of the Bible is about restoring creation, not escaping from it. When Jesus returns, the separation caused by sin will be fully healed and God's people will live in perfect peace. So, as we wait upon Christ's final return, we can begin to usher in heaven today. Let's live as citizens of heaven and conduct ourselves in a manner worthy of the Gospel message (Philippians 1:27).

Jesus, thank you for making me part of your Kingdom here on earth. Empower me to spread your message of hope as I live out the Gospel message. Help me understand your plan for my life and my world. I ask you to grow my faith and teach me to trust you with aspects of the future I don't understand. Give me a greater sensitivity to your Spirit as I seek to dwell in your presence until you return again. Motivate me to conduct myself in a manner worthy of my calling and give me the boldness to stand up for the cause of Christ. In your name, Amen.

Personal Reflection

Read John 14 in the light of what we've discussed over the last three days. Then consider whether God has led you to shift or change your view of heaven. How has your understanding of heaven altered, if at all, and how does that impact your walk with God?

Scan the QR code for passages of Scripture

_____

_____

_____

_____

_____

_____

Day 83

Day 84
Crab-tastic

Many years ago when Asher was in middle school, he adopted two tiny pet crabs. He carefully curated their habitat and tended to them diligently. Shortly after, however, Asher went out of town for a week-long camp. He was concerned about his new pets, but I assured him that I would care for them while he was away.

In one of my most stellar parenting moments ever, I completely forgot about the crabs. As soon as Asher returned home, he found the remnants of two dead crustaceans, who had attempted to eat one another as they starved to death. Although Asher has forgiven me, he has never let me forget my horrendously unfulfilled promise.

Our Lord knows that we are prone to make mistakes and renege on commitments, so he exhorts us to be careful about making vows. Such warnings are found in both the Old and New Testaments. Whether we make a promise to God or another human, the Lord commands, "A man who makes a vow to the LORD or makes a pledge under oath must never break it. He must do exactly what he said he would do," (Numbers 30:2). Jesus warns similarly,

> *You have also heard that our ancestors were told, "You must not break your vows; you must carry out the vows you make to the LORD." But I say, do not make any vows! Do not say, "By heaven!" because heaven is God's throne. And do not say, "By the*

earth!" because the earth is his footstool. And do not say, "By Jerusalem!" for Jerusalem is the city of the great King. Do not even say, "By my head!" for you can't turn one hair white or black. Just say a simple, "Yes, I will," or "No, I won't." Anything beyond this is from the evil one.

Matthew 5:33–37

Jesus teaches that our word should be so trustworthy that we don't need formal vows. Additionally, he knows that we are fallible humans and, thus, seeks to protect us from the consequences of breaking an oath. As Christ followers, the integrity of our word reflects upon our Savior. If we renege on commitments, or even worse, default upon formal agreements, our lack of integrity reflects poorly upon our Savior and our fellow believers.

We can avoid negative outcomes by carefully considering each commitment. From the biggest promise to the smallest task, we should seek the wisdom of the Lord *before* we say "yes." In matters of great consequence, we might need to consult trusted advisors or mentors while we take time to consider the best possible decision. In this way, our "yes" can be "yes," our "no" can be "no," and our Lord can be honored. Let's heed the advice of Jesus and avoid any crab-tastic disasters in the future!

Lord, thank you for honoring every commitment you made on this earth, to the point of death for my sins. Help me learn from your faithful example so that I can bring honor to you and your Kingdom. Give me the diligence and discipline to fulfill every agreement I make. Teach me to make wise decisions and learn to say "no" when needed. Guide me as I seek your will regarding how I should spend my time and energy. Give me greater wisdom in decisions, both large and small. In Jesus' name, Amen.

Personal Reflection

Prayerfully meditate on your track record with promises and commitments. Are you diligent to fulfill your word or do you consider follow-through optional? Do you have good intentions of fulfilling your promises, but often get sidetracked and forget? As you reflect, look for patterns and solutions. If you struggle to fulfill your commitments, consider why. Ask God to reveal one avenue of discipline for you to practice in regard to your promises. For example, do you need to learn to say "no," do you need to be more proactive, or do you need to create reminders to help you remember your obligations? Write your thoughts below.

_____

_____

_____

_____

_____

_____

_____

_____

_____

_____

Day 84

_____

_____

_____

_____

_____

_____

_____

_____

_____

_____

_____

_____

_____

_____

_____

_____

_____

_____

_____

_____

Day 85
Spiritual Ecosystem

Recently some of my friends gifted me with a terrarium. A new avenue of gardening for me, I quickly became obsessed with learning everything about these living works of art. The two primary types of terraria are closed and open. Since open terraria are similar to potted plants, I'll tell you specifically about the closed version.

A closed terrarium is a self-contained ecosystem composed of water, plants, microfauna, and light. Rocks and decorative features are often present, but not required. Each of the other elements are necessary in order for the ecosystem to live, grow, and thrive. The clear walls of the terrarium allow light to enter, which promotes photosynthesis and growth among the plants. The sealed container also fosters a water system in miniature, in which water evaporates, condenses, and keeps the plants nourished. However, the humid biological environment also creates perfect conditions for the growth of mold. Thus microfauna (tiny bugs) are necessary to keep fungal growth under control.

Each element of the ecosystem must be introduced in the right amount in order for the terrarium to thrive. For example, too much water will cause the plants to rot, too little will cause the plants to wither. In addition, the wrong types of microfauna will eat your plants. Some types of microfauna, such as ladybugs, will even consume the other species of microfauna. The amount of light must also be monitored, as too much light will cook everything in your ecosystem.

The careful balance of the terrarium ecosystem reminds me of the manner in which our spiritual life functions. Just as each element in the terrarium is essential to the health of the whole, the health of our spiritual life depends upon a variety of elements. The prophet Micah offered a concise statement of desired components while also delivering an extensive list of elements that will ruin our spiritual ecosystem. He taught,

What can we bring to the Lord?
Should we bring him burnt offerings?
Should we bow before God Most High
with offerings of yearling calves?
Should we offer him thousands of rams
and ten thousand rivers of olive oil?
Should we sacrifice our firstborn children
to pay for our sins?
No, O people, the Lord has told you what is good,
and this is what he requires of you:
to do what is right, to love mercy,
and to walk humbly with your God.
Fear the Lord if you are wise!
His voice calls to everyone in Jerusalem:
The armies of destruction are coming;
the Lord is sending them.
What shall I say about the homes of the wicked
filled with treasures gained by cheating?
What about the disgusting practice
of measuring out grain with dishonest measures?
How can I tolerate your merchants
who use dishonest scales and weights?

The rich among you have become wealthy
through extortion and violence.
Your citizens are so used to lying
that their tongues can no longer tell the truth.

Micah 6:6–12

Let me draw your attention to several points from this passage. First, although God calls us to return the tithe, giving offerings without tending to the condition of our heart throws the whole ecosystem off balance and creates a self-centered, narcissistic faith. Second, accumulating wealth dishonestly, seeking our own benefit at the expense of others, or harming the less fortunate will absolutely destroy our spiritual health. A thriving spiritual life consists of loving God so much that we serve others and obey him out of the overflow of that love. Third, just as the terrarium needs certain elements to thrive, the essential elements of our spiritual walk include living uprightly, loving faithfully, and walking humbly before God. Because our spiritual ecosystem is filled with his life-giving presence, each element complements and benefits the other. Which elements of your environment might need adjusting today?

Father, thank you for equipping me to live a well-balanced spiritual life. Help me foster each element that I need to thrive and eliminate every hindrance to my health. Reveal any areas in which I am unbalanced and teach me to find optimal measures of obedience, love, and humility. Empower me to bless the people in my life rather than seeking my own interests. Give me a heart to serve you well and see others thrive so that my own flourishing is an outgrowth of spiritual health. In Jesus' name, Amen.

Personal Reflection

Prayerfully meditate on the essential elements of your spiritual growth (living uprightly, loving faithfully, and walking humbly before God) as well as the elements that will destroy your health (accumulating wealth dishonestly, seeing our own benefit at the expense of others, and harming/ignoring the less fortunate). Choose one essential element and one destructive element to focus on today. How can you cultivate more of the virtue that you need and minimize the element that hinders your health? Write your thoughts below.

_____

_____

_____

_____

_____

_____

_____

_____

_____

_____

_____

_____

Day 86
Deeply Rooted

One afternoon, Asher and Abel were helping me move some potted plants. As Abel was transporting an especially large pothos, a viny houseplant with heart-shaped leaves, he stumbled and dropped the plant. The pot shattered and fragments went everywhere. We cleaned up the dirt and threw away the fragments of the ceramic pot, but since pothos are quite resilient, I saved the plant for repotting.

As I was later repotting the plant, I had to choose which pieces to save and which to discard. One particular stem was completely barren, but it had a large root bundle. I debated whether to preserve it, but since pothos grow quickly, I decided to keep the stem. Over the following weeks, I kept a close eye on the leafless shoot. It was still alive, but it simply refused to grow new leaves. I almost uprooted it numerous times but felt vested in its preservation. Finally, after months had passed, a tiny leaf began to emerge, then another, and another.

As the plant grew, God reminded me of just how vital our spiritual roots are. Paul teaches,

> *So please don't lose heart because of my trials here. I am suffering for you, so you should feel honored. When I think of all this, I fall to my knees and pray to the Father, the Creator of everything in heaven and on earth. I pray that from his glorious, unlimited*

resources he will empower you with inner strength through his Spirit. Then Christ will make his home in your hearts as you trust in him. Your roots will grow down into God's love and keep you strong. And may you have the power to understand, as all God's people should, how wide, how long, how high, and how deep his love is. May you experience the love of Christ, though it is too great to understand fully. Then you will be made complete with all the fullness of life and power that comes from God.

Ephesians 3:13–20

The key to a thriving life in Christ is to cultivate deep roots of faith. In seasons of trial, we might fail to bear fruit. We might struggle to survive. Yet, if our lives are rooted in the love of God, our souls will remain strong. New growth may take months, years, or even decades, but our perseverance will eventually bear fruit.

Yet, our roots must be strong *before* we are faced with trial. We must be rooted in Christ so that when other foundations are stripped away, our faith nourishes our soul and keeps us secure until we reach more abundant seasons. We may never fully understand our seasons of struggle, but we don't have to! Let's simply thank Jesus and grow our roots deep into his love.

Jesus, thank you for loving me unconditionally and empowering me to withstand every trial. Help me to experience your love fully and live my faith purposefully. I pray you would grow my roots more deeply into the healthy soil of faith. Forgive me for doubting you in seasons of trial instead of seeking nourishment from you. Help me learn from past mistakes so that I can weather difficult seasons with greater faith and fortitude in the future.

Teach me to be patient in seasons of outward dormancy and inner healing. In your name, Amen.

Personal Reflection

Reflect on your response to seasons of trial. Do your spiritual roots help you endure without falling apart? Or do you doubt God's goodness and shun his love? Do you experience frustration with seasons that lack outward fruit and productivity? Or do you lean into the inward work of God in your heart. Prayerfully identify one area of potential growth, write it below, and begin to cultivate it at the earliest opportunity.

Day 87
Root Rot

Near the beginning of the summer, I had planted flowers in a new pot near the front door of my house. I looked forward to seeing them grow and bloom. But they didn't. I was confused, because I knew they had plenty of water and the right amount of sunlight. I watched helplessly as the plant began to wither and die.

Around the same time, I noticed an awful smell in the same area. Day by day, the odor grew stronger until I finally traced the source of the smell to my flowerpot! And as soon as I did, I understood the problem. You see, most potted plants need holes in the bottom of their pots so that excess water can run out. If surplus water has no outlet, it will become stagnant and cause the roots of the plant to rot. And sure enough, as soon as I drilled holes into the bottom of the pot and ran clean water through the soil, the flowers began to thrive.

The flowerpot situation reminds me of a principle found in Proverbs 11:25: "The person who blesses will be blessed, and the one who waters will be watered," (my translation). When we allow God's living water to flow *through* us, we refresh others and we, ourselves, are refreshed. When we make sacrifices for our friends, encourage our peers, or serve our family, we are blessed and enriched. Even when we think we don't have the time or energy, even when our kindness isn't returned immediately, God will bless our investment. Just like the loaves and fishes in the hands of Jesus, our Lord will multiply that which we entrust to him. Whether we are short on time, financial resources, emotional capacity, or physical energy, we can't afford *not* to let God manage our gifts for us.

When we hold everything close to the chest, growth comes to a halt. Just like my poor plant sitting in rancid water, when God's living water isn't flowing *through* us, we become puny and lifeless. We might even be consuming plenty of God's living water through Bible study, prayer and/or church attendance, but we will still become stagnant if we aren't serving others. Let's bless and refresh the people in our lives with the living water of God, then watch our own faith flourish and bloom.

Jesus, thank you for pouring out your life on my behalf. Conform me to your image so that I'm a pure vessel for the living water you offer. I ask you to fill me up so that I can be poured out on behalf of others. Help me surrender every blessing to you so that I can be a blessing to my family and friends. Equip me to serve and encourage the people around me in meaningful ways. Most importantly, empower me to share the Gospel at every opportunity. In your name, Amen.

Personal Reflection

Be intentional to bless and refresh the people in your life today.

_____

_____

_____

_____

_____

_____

Day 88
Root Bound

Cooler weather is in the air. My gardening season is starting to wind down, and it's the time of year that I always feel a bit of frustration with my garden, or at least the plants that are in pots. They grow all summer long. They grow big and beautiful. But then around late August and early September, many of them start to wither, no matter how much water I give them and no matter how carefully I tend to them.

What happens is that, just as the visible part above the soil grows, so also the roots beneath the soil grow, and grow, and grow, until they simply run out of space inside the pot. They become "root bound," and when a plant becomes root bound, the roots can't properly absorb water and nutrients. And the more root bound the plant gets, the unhealthier it becomes.

We can encounter a similar situation in our spiritual lives. Paul says, "Don't let anyone capture you with empty philosophies and high-sounding nonsense that come from human thinking and from the spiritual powers of this world, rather than from Christ," (Colossians 2:8). When we allow ourselves to rely on human wisdom instead of faith in Christ, we start to get bound up. And just as root bound plants get twisted up and start to strangle themselves, when we allow the traits of earthly wisdom to creep into our lives, they gradually crowd out our relationship with Jesus. Earthly wisdom prevents us from absorbing the living water and nutrients that God provides for us. This starvation of faith becomes a vicious cycle in which we become more and more unhealthy if we don't deal with the "root issues."

James helps us remain healthy by providing a well-rounded description of both earthly and Godly wisdom in chapter 3 of his epistle. He tells us that earthly wisdom consists of envy, selfish ambition, boasting, and denying the truth, all of which lead to disorder and evil (James 3:14–16). He then describes how to avoid getting bound up as he encourages us to live out godly wisdom, which consists of purity, humility, gentleness, friendliness, compassion, goodness, authenticity, and peaceableness (James 3:17–18). Paul, similarly, teaches us that if we continue to emulate Christ, nothing will be able to bind us up. He says, "And now, just as you accepted Christ Jesus as your Lord, you must continue to follow him. Let your roots grow down into him, and let your lives be built on him. Then your faith will grow strong in the truth you were taught, and you will overflow with thankfulness," (Colossians 2:6–7) When we build our lives on faith in Christ, our roots grow deeper, stronger, and healthier. Our relationship with Jesus gives us freedom, so our roots have space to continue growing and flourishing.

Jesus, thank you for the forgiveness and salvation that provides healthy soil in which my roots can grow. Help me live out your wisdom and never get bound up by the ideals and thought patterns of the world. Use me to show your compassion and goodness to the world. Give me opportunities to plant seeds that bring peace and freedom to others. In your name, Amen.

Personal Reflection

Consider the traits of earthly wisdom and heavenly wisdom. Are you allowing yourself to be bound up by envy, selfish ambition, boasting, or deception? Which traits of heavenly wisdom do you need to cultivate more of in your life: peacefulness, gentleness, friendliness, compassion, or service?

_____

_____

_____

_____

_____

_____

_____

_____

_____

_____

_____

_____

_____

_____

_____

Day 89
Rooting Around

Over the last few days, we've meditated upon different aspects of roots. We've talked about how deep roots keep our souls healthy even in seasons of hardship. We've discussed steps necessary to maintain healthy roots, like allowing God's living water to pour through us as we serve others. And we've discussed maintaining healthy roots by guarding against earthly wisdom. Only by continually nourishing our roots with Godly wisdom can we remain healthy and deeply rooted.

Since we are on the topic, I decided to dig a little more deeply to see what other spiritual truths God might teach us through roots. (The devotional series is called *Rooted* & Flourishing, after all!) As I began to research, I learned that roots are even more fascinating than I'd thought. The function of roots extends beyond the basic tasks of delivering water and nutrients to plants. Some scientists go so far as to identify the root system as the brain of a plant.

Roots are like a brain in that they sense the environment around them. (They even look a bit like a brain if you remove the soil.) They detect water and nutrients and move toward those sources. Many plants and trees can survive drought because the roots are able to seek out distant sources of water. Some desert-dwelling trees, such as the Shepherd's Tree in Africa and the Texas Mesquite can grow roots 200 feet deep!

Recent research convincingly suggests that trees can communicate with one another through their roots. Root filaments connect through underground fungal networks to share nutrients and resources. Most fascinating of all "trees send chemical, hormonal and slow-pulsing electrical signals, which scientists are just beginning to decipher." What are the trees saying to one another? We don't yet know, but we hope to find out!

So, what spiritual lessons can we appropriate from our newly learned facts about roots? Allow me to suggest a few. First, deep, healthy roots will help us find sources of nourishment. They don't simply sustain us through seasons of hardship, they help us maintain a trajectory of health and growth. Second, our roots are more than just spiritual intuition. Healthy roots are like a spiritual brain, helping us discern between Godly wisdom and worldly wisdom. Third, our roots are the means by which we communicate with our Father. As we share our thoughts and emotions with him, he helps us think clearly and make wise decisions. As Peter says, "You already know these things, dear friends. So be on guard; then you will not be carried away . . . and lose your own secure footing [or healthy roots]. Rather, you must grow in the grace and knowledge of our Lord and Savior Jesus Christ," (2 Peter 3:17). Like the spiritual ecosystem we discussed several days ago, caring for our roots involves a healthy balance of wisdom, knowledge, virtue, and faith in God. Let's grow our roots more deeply into Jesus every day.

Lord, thank you for giving me the capacity to learn and grow. Help me to diligently pursue a greater knowledge of you and a greater faith in your promises. I repent of ignoring my own growth and health. Equip me to discern between earthly wisdom and heavenly wisdom as I seek to grow stronger in the foundations of my faith. Teach me to seek your presence and guidance so that I can think clearly and continue to grow even in seasons of hardship and spiritual drought. Show me areas in which my roots are weak or in which my spiritual ecosystem is unbalanced. Grow me healthier in every area of my life so that I can bring greater glory and honor to your Name. Amen.

Personal Reflection

Meditate on the idea of your spiritual roots as the brain of your soul. How can you extend your roots more deeply into the Lord by growing in your knowledge of him or your communication with him? Do you need to spend more time conversing with your Father and seeking his guidance in prayer? Do you need to be more intentional about your study of Scripture and your knowledge of the Bible? Or are your roots lacking depth in some other area? Determine one action step you can take this week to grow your roots more deeply in God.

Day 89

Day 90
Seasons Change

As we draw our summer volume of devotionals to a close, I'd like to return once more to the theme of changing seasons. Just as the seasons of the natural world transition from one to the next, so also the seasons of our life transform, develop, and shift. As we move into the autumn, perhaps you are in a season of harvesting that which you planted in the spring and summer. Or perhaps you are even now planting seeds that will sprout in the future.

Because each season of life is different, change is inevitable. In fact, change is one of the few constants we can expect in this life. A vital part of our existence, change can help us draw closer to our Father and grow in wisdom so long as we continue to seek him. Isaiah expresses a similar principle as he instructs,

Listen to me;
listen, and pay close attention.
Does a farmer always plow and never sow?
Is he forever cultivating the soil and never planting?
Does he not finally plant his seeds—
black cumin, cumin, wheat, barley, and emmer
wheat—
each in its proper way,
and each in its proper place?
The farmer knows just what to do,

for God has given him understanding.

. . .

The Lord of Heaven's Armies is a wonderful teacher,
and he gives the farmer great wisdom.
Isaiah 28:23–25, 29

As we seek God's guidance, he reveals his will for each season and equips us to fulfill his purposes. So, let's do just that and seek his wisdom as we prepare for our next season. But first, let's not rush forward so quickly that we fail to see the fresh blessings of today.

Heavenly Father, thank you for the multitude of blessings you shower upon me. I praise you for your mercies in the past, present, and future. Teach me to recognize the blessings you have for me in each season of my life. Give me the wisdom to understand your purpose for my current season and prepare me to trust you in future seasons. Help me accept change without fear and view each phase of life as an opportunity to draw closer to you. In Jesus' name, Amen.

Personal Reflection

Prayerfully meditate on the last several months of devotionals. You may even want to flip backward through the pages and read some of your notes. Take extra time today (perhaps tomorrow as well) to celebrate your growth and identify next steps. Organize your thoughts into three lists and write your notes below. First, celebrate areas in which you are flourishing. How have you become more healthy, mature, and established? What might you be harvesting from seeds you planted in a previous season of life? Second, identify areas in which 3you are currently growing. What strategies are you implementing in order to become healthier? What habits or patterns of thought are you allowing God to prune from your life? Third, identify a few opportunities for future growth. What seeds can you plant today in order to produce healthy fruit in future seasons of your life? If you read the autumn volume of Rooted & Flourishing, you've completed this exercise once already. So, before you write your thoughts today, refer back to your notes from the autumn. Ask God to help you see how you've grown as well as any areas you might need to keep tending the soil and planting new seeds. If you haven't yet read the autumn devotionals, be sure to take good notes today so you can refer back to them in the future.

_____

_____

_____

_____

_____

_____

_____

_____

_____

_____

_____